DON KILA

and
MALIK KILAM
PRESENTS:

Name Some Of the marks that were put upon the Moors of Northwest, by the European Nations in 1774:

Negro Black, Colored and Ethiopia.

What is meant by the Word Negro?

Negro, a name given to a river in West Africa by the Moors, because it contained black water.

What Is Meant by the word Black?

Black, according to science means death.

What does the word Colored mean?

Colored means anything that has been painted, stained, vanished, or dyed.

What Does Ethiopia mean?

Ethiopia means something divided.

Can A man be a Negro Black, Colored and Ethiopian?

No.

Why?

Because man is made in the Imagine and the Likeness of God, Allah.

What Title Does Satan Give Himself?

God.

Will you define the word White?

White Means Purity, Purity means God, and God means the Ruler of the Land.

(Excerpt from the Islam Koran Questions For Moors Divinely Prepared by the founder of the Moor Science Temple of America Noble Drew Ali)

WARNING

OFFICIAL
PRIVATE
PLANNING

MALIK KILAM

1. Nationality
2. Status correction
3. 1099 OID Education
4. Personal Debt Elimination
5. Court Elimination
6. Bonds, Stocks, Notes & Securities
7. I Self Law Am Master

1.   Nationality

The Vatican Owns Everything

On 18 November 1302, Pope Boniface VIII issued the Papal Bull called "Unum Sanctum."

Aside from all that was written, the bull ends with the following statement:

"Furthermore, we declare, we proclaim, we define that it is absolutely necessary for salvation that every human creature be subject to the Roman Pontiff."

Since the bull declared that the Roman Pontiff has supreme control over the material world, he states that the body (our body) is governed by the soul and the soul is governed by the ruler of the spiritual, therefore - the Roman Pontiff is Governor of both Soul and body.

Basically, what it is saying is that all of the Souls in the world belong to the Roman Catholic Church and apparently, at least in theory, they do ... because no one has dared challenged their claim. Your birth certificate is the title of the Soul that they own in their registries. They have registered you and that is the title to your Soul. Like the bank holds the title to your car because you are indebted to them. In fact, your Social Security card is issued to you with your name in all capital letters ... which indicates chattel to a Corporation. We are inventory.

The Roman Catholic Church has a very long history of tyranny and oppression dating back to the very beginning of it's organization. Because of their desire to control through their crusades and inquisitions, they decided they would create the first Express Trust, called "Unam Sanctum" which was written on a papal bull and

placed in their vault. Remember, there are 66 miles of shelving in that vault locked away underground beneath the Vatican.

On the papal bull, it says that all of the souls in the world belong to the Roman Catholic Church and they technically do, because no one has challenged their claim. Your Birth Certificate is essentially the title of the Soul that they own in their registries. They have registered you and that is the title to your Soul. Given that there is a small group of

Global Elite who control all the world's finances, military, and ecclesiastical resources, this would not be too difficult to believe.

The Inquisition began because many people were waking up to the tyranny and oppression of the Roman Catholic Church in the early 1300's. The RCC killed these people due to their need to control humanity. And kill they did. In the millions it is estimated. And it wasn't pretty. Not even Stephen King could come up with some of the ways they "tortured and disposed" of people who opposed them. 200 years later during the Renaissance, the Hermetica (based upon the Ancient Wisdom and teachings of Hermes) was available, which is where the Bible draws all of its inspiration from, along with previous civilizations and their rituals and beliefs. This knowledge was also suppressed by the RCC ... for centuries.

Global Elite families control the Vatican and the Corporation (the incorporation of the Apostle Peter). They also control the US Military, and the London Financial District - all three of which are independent city/states. The control center is the Crown Temple Syndicate. The Washington DC private corporation Federal Estate is actually owned and controlled by the London Crown Temple Syndicate. The Syndicate, through the House of Windsor, owns approximately 1/6 of the Earths land surface. But I digress ...

In 325 CE, the emperor, Constantine the Great, made a donation to his Pope, Sylvester saying, "Saint Peter is the Apostle of Jesus of whom Jesus gave this kingdom of Earth to, therefore we are going to claim taxes." We pay taxes to Rome, the Khazarian and Venetian Black Nobility elite families based on a fictional document from Constantine issued the year of the First Council of Nicea and the creation of what has become modern day Christianity.

Because of a decree written by Pope Nicholas V in 1455, the RCC owns everything, Even what you think you might own such as your car, house or even the pair of shoes you are wearing belongs to the RCC (in their twisted minds). The UNITED STATES is a wholly owned subsidiary of the Crown and a full-blown Corporation. It began as "The Virginia Company," and then ultimately became, "The United States of America Corporation." If you do a quick search of the United States Codes it clearly states on **28 U.S.C. 3002 (15)** "United States" means—

(A)
a Federal corporation;
(B)

an agency, department, commission, board, or other entity of the <u>United States</u>; or

(C)
an instrumentality of the <u>United States</u>.

*The **corporation** was created for the District of Columbia, aka Washington, D.C. (not even a **state**), via the Act of 1871.*
*THE **UNITED STATES** corporation operates under private international law with their own **corporate** constitution*

The <u>papal bull</u> **Aeterni regis** [English: "Eternal king's"] was issued on 21 June 1481 by <u>Pope Sixtus IV</u>. It confirmed the substance of the <u>Treaty of Alcáçovas</u>, reiterating that treaty's confirmation of <u>Castile</u> in its possession of the <u>Canary Islands</u> and its granting to <u>Portugal</u> all further territorial acquisitions made by Christian powers in Africa and eastward to the Indies.

11 February 1531 – Convocation grants Henry VIII the title of Supreme Head of the English Church

What is a "Ces tui Qui Trust" (pronounce set-a-kay) and why should you care?

In 1666, in London, during the black plague, and great fires of london Parliament enacted an act, behind closed doors, called Cestui Que Vie Act 1666.

http://www.opsi.gov.uk/RevisedStatute...

The act being debated the Cestui Qui act was to subrogate the rights of men and women, meaning all men and women were declared dead, lost at sea/beyond the sea. (back then operating in admiralty law, the law of the sea, so lost at sea).

The state (of London) took custody of everybody and their property into a trust, the state became the trustee/husband holding all titles to the people and property, until a living man comes back to reclaim those titles and can also claim damages. (Reclaim using UCC 1 and PPSA)

The rule of the use of CAPITAL LETTERS used in a NAME: when CAPITAL letters re used anywhere in a NAME this always refers to a LEGAL ENTITY/FICTION, COMPANY or CORPORATION no exceptions.

e.g. John DOE or Doe: JANE (PASSPORT, DRIVER LICENSE, MARRIAGE CERTIFICATE and BIRTH CERTIFICATE)

CEST TUI QUE TRUST: (pronounced setakay) common term in NEW ZEALAND and AUSTRALIA or STRAWMAN common term in USA or CANADA is a LEGAL ENTITY/FICTION created and owned by the GOVERNMENT whom created it. I repeat owned by the GOVERNMENT.

Legally, we are considered to be a FICTION, a concept or idea expressed as a NAME, a symbol. That LEGAL PERSON has no consciousness; it is a juristic PERSON, ENS LEGIS, a NAME/word written on a piece of paper.

This traces back to 1666, London is a state, just like Vatican is a state, just like Washington DC is a state. The Crown is an unincorporated association. Why unincorporated, its private, the temple bar is in London, every lawyer called to the "bar" swears allegiance to the temple bar. You can't get called, without swearing this allegiance. The Crown already owns North America and everything in it.

Your only way out is to reclaim your dead entity (strawman) that the Crown created, become the trustee of the cest tui qui trust and remove yourself from the admiralty law that holds you in custody.

The subrogation of your rights

When London burned the subrogation of mens and womens rights occurred.

The responsible act passed... CQV act 1666 meant all men and women of UK were declared dead and lost beyond the seas. The state took everybody and everybody's property into trust. The state takes control until a living man or woman comes back and claims their titles by proving they are alive and claims for damages can be made.

This is why you always need representation when involved in legal matters, because you're dead. The legal fiction is a construct on paper, an estate in trust. When you get a bill or summons from court it is always in capital letters, similar to tomb stones in grave yards. Capital letters signify death. They are writing to the dead legal fiction. A legal fiction was created when someone informed the government that there was a new vessel in town, based upon your birth. Birth certificates are issued at birth, just as ships are given berth certificates.

Your mother has a birth canal, just like a ship. All this information relates to how the general public are still legally tied. Through admiralty law, through this ancient legal construct we can be easily controlled. Learning about your legal fiction helps you to unlock yourself. Otherwise you are just a vessel floating on the sea of commerce. It is possible to be free from financial stress and debt.

Parents are tricked into registering the birth of their babies. In about 1837 the Births, Deaths and Marriages act was formed in UK and the post of registrar general was established. His job was to collect all the data from the churches which held the records of birth.

Regis - from queen or crown. All people are seen to be in custody of," The Crown". This allows people to function in commerce and to accept the benefits provided by state.

So we are in custody. Worldwide - under the IMF the majority of people are fed, sheltered and provided for, however now it is the system that is benefitting while many are suffering, are poorly fed, housed and water is contaminated. Many people are now getting sick and dying as a result - not to mention that as people evolve, they now seek to be independent of any system that seeks to control or oppress and harms the earth that this is all taking place on.

We have legally elected representatives. We have to understand who we are as men and women and how we can relate in the system.

The City of London is a centre for markets, where merchants work. Then there is mercantile law. It comes from Admiralty. Look at the symbols in the City of London that relate to Admiralty.

Our national banks are not our banks. The private shareholders from the private banks own the banks. It is all private, not public as we are led to believe. "OF" also means "without", eg. The bank without England. Private banks issue private currency.

With WWI a change happened where money was not backed by gold or silver anymore, it is now based on peoples labour. People are now pledged to the IMF as the surety to pay back the creditors in the global bankruptcy. Men and women are not bankrupt, they are the only source of credit. The public is bankrupt.

Regarding the currency that gets issued at the Bank of England, people are the gold or the treasure. The government issues bonds or treasury bills that are bought by investors. The money goes back into the economy in order to pay for the people to build things, e.g. an Olympic Stadium. However, the people are paying taxes for the privilege of using someone else's currency and paying back the principal and the interest on the original loan that was given against the treasury bonds, bills and notes. It is a private corporation that will own the Olympic stadium, be responsible for running it, be able to sell commercial rights, yet the people are actually the ones who own it and should be profiting from it. However, principal and interest is coming through the people in order to raise the money.

So where you have commerce and money, you also have "justice". You need to understand the bankruptcy before you can understand the judiciary. You need to accept the bankruptcy. We have accepted the claim to accept the summons. There is an obligation to accept any liability which has been created. All you can do is accept the bankruptcy. We are operating in admiralty. A not guilty plea dishonours the bankruptcy. The strawman, aka legal fiction is always guilty. It needs to be accepted for value. Barristers and solicitors make a living out of creating controversy. By creating a controversy you become liable for the case.

Honour and dishonour. To remain in honour you have to accept a claim and settle it. Then you add conditions. I accept on proof of claim and proof of loss. This gives the liability back to them. The legal fiction is always guilty. Only in the high courts, can the real man or woman appear. Games are played on courts; hence the name court is a game with actors (acting on acts). It has to be treated as a game and just business. Court room dramas are misinformation. In the public, we are operating in bankruptcy and you receive benefits. It takes a lot of time, effort and study to use these tools. You have to be prepared to go fully through the process, get the right tool out of your toolbox at the right time. People need to learn how to act as creditors.

In summary...

- Money is backed by labour.
- We cannot exchange it fairly for gold or silver.

- Capitalisation of "name" means a dead entity, a legal fiction.
- Know who you are, you are not your strawman or dead fictitious entity.
- Learn how to become a creditor in commerce.

All the best with this!!! Contact us for more information about what we are discovering - sincere inquiries by men and women who are committed to the road of a Sui Juris

An intro into the ideas of how your (entity, strawman, allcaps name) was created. In 1666 an act of parliament created during the black plague, and great fires of london , behind closed doors, was called Cestui Que Vie Act 1666. Which Ties directly to the Social Security Trust for the public debt dealing directly with any country's National Public Debt and Bankruptcy.

The act being debated was the Cestui Qui act which was to subrogate the rights of men and women, meaning all men and women were declared dead, lost at sea/beyond the sea. This was done during a crisis. The state took custody of everybody and their property into a trust, the Cestui Qui trust, the state became the trustee/husband holding all titles to the people and property, until a living man comes back to reclaim those titles and can also claim damages.

The Cestui Qui act or Trust created is an ALL-CAPITALIZED NAME, a 'dead entity' who had all his belongings put into a trust. This act still exists, and this trust still exists.

This is how it started. The videos by Don Kilam and Malik Kilam Legacy on youtube all speak about this subject. The basis of how bankers use the law to hijack an all-caps name that you didn't even know existed.

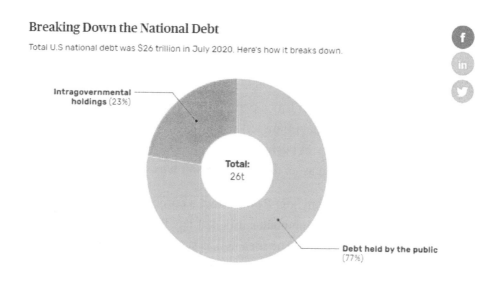

Breaking Down the National Debt

Total U.S national debt was $26 trillion in July 2020. Here's how it breaks down.

Intragovernmental holdings (23%)

Total: 26t

Debt held by the public (77%)

Chart: The Balance • Source: U.S. Department of the Treasury

the balance

The U.S. debt reached a new high of $27 trillion as of Oct. 1, 2020.[1] Most headlines focus on how much the United States owes China, one of the largest foreign owners. What many people don't know is that the Social Security Trust Fund, also known as your retirement money, owns most of the national debt. According to thebalance.com $21 Trillion is What Is Due to the Public and through this book we will be showing you of many ways to access what is already due upon the public and the Social Security Trust.

If you were born on earth, if you have a birth certificate and social security number, this applies to you. The only way to claim your trust and get free from admiralty law, is to understand who you really are, and that admiralty law does not apply to you, but in order to get free you must do some homework, file forms and know how commerce applies to you.

Here's a term that describes a situation when a court makes something out of nothing: It's called **legal fiction**. This jargon refers to the law's ability to decree that something that's not necessarily true is true. It's somewhat like a person in a discussion agreeing to accept an opinion as fact for the sake of argument in order to move the discussion along. Legal fiction helps to move proceedings along.

A sterling example of legal fiction is what's called **corporate personhood**. Think about it: A corporation isn't a person. It's a business, a pool of investors' money used to conduct transactions and hopefully make a profit. But in order to determine the legality of business proceedings, the legal fiction of treating a corporation as an **artificial person** was created.

This concept isn't new. In ancient Roman law, a corporation was considered a **juristic person**: a single, nonhuman entity that legally represented a group of many people [source: Sherman]. The idea makes sense; after all, a corporation is made up of people's financial contributions.

But a corporation is more superhuman than human. It can function beyond the natural limits of age that govern humans, and as such can produce dividends for its investors, whose stock certificates can be willed and passed down as part of their estates. A corporation doesn't die with its originator -- it can live indefinitely (so long as it's profitable). Nor does a corporation need the same things that an actual person does. Corporations don't require food or water, and they can't feel pain [source: Hartmann].

The laws that govern people take our human weaknesses into account. For example, our prison system is designed to incarcerate the human body. You can't imprison a corporation, though. So granting human treatment to nonhuman corporations is tricky: It's like breathing life into a superhuman that can't feel pain and, after setting him free, hoping for the best.

It would make sense that in dealing with corporations, the United States would tread lightly and limit the power that these artificial persons have. This hasn't necessarily been the case, however. In fact, in the United States, corporations have the same protections under the Constitution that humans do.

The 14th Amendment and Artificial Personhood

So how did corporations come to enjoy the same Constitutional protections that people do? It all started with a court reporter. In his book, "Unequal protection: The rise of Corporate Dominance and the Theft of Human Rights," author Thom Hartmann describes the situation that gave rise to Constitutional protection for corporations.

Since corporations had been viewed as artificial persons for millennia, the debate over whether they should be afforded the same rights as humans had been raging long before the **14th Amendment** was adopted. Thomas Jefferson had suggested explicit language to govern corporate entities, like requiring maximum life spans, be put into the Constitution. His stipulations didn't make the cut, however. And once the 14th Amendment was created, the Constitution actually expanded -- rather than limited -- the scope of corporations' power.

The 14th Amendment was adopted in 1868, and it gave the federal government ultimate power over the states in respect to the rights of newly freed slaves. The amendment sought to overturn state-level legislation that was being created to limit the liberties of freedmen after the Civil War. The federal government circumvented each one of these laws with a broad sweep: Through the 14th Amendment, Congress granted equal protection under the law to every person [source: Library of Congress]. That last word is important, since in the eyes of the law, a corporation is an artificial person.

While the 14th Amendment opened the door for corporate Constitutional rights, the issue wasn't really addressed until 1868. A dispute over whether a county has the right to tax a corporation turned out to settle this much larger issue in a very strange way.

In the case of Santa Clara County v. Southern Pacific Railroad, the Supreme Court decided that only the state that charters a corporation can tax it. This decision upheld the long-standing custom in America of state governance of corporations. It's the state that grants a corporation its **charter** -- its license to do business -- and it's up to the state to tax and regulate the corporation.

But a note written by the court reporter at the heading of the decision went further than that. Although another, private note from the Chief Justice said that the court had purposely avoided the issue of Constitutional corporate protection, the reporter chose to make his own addition to the records. He noted that the court had decided that corporations are persons under the 14th Amendment, and as such are subject to the same protections under the law as anyone else [source: Hartmann].

What's strange, Hartmann points out, is that the justices hadn't ruled that way at all. Even fishier, the court reporter was a former railroad president [source: Hartmann]. Ultimately, since it was a **headnote** (a commentary prefix to the court record) written by the reporter, it didn't constitute law. But it did set precedent. Two years later, this idea was upheld in another case: Pembina Consolidated Mining and Milling Co. v. Pennsylvania [source: Aljalian].

Just how much Constitutional protection corporations should be afforded is still being hammered out today, court case by court case. Examples in the past have been Nike and Wal Mart as said to be running sweat shops

Right to a Nationality and Statelessness

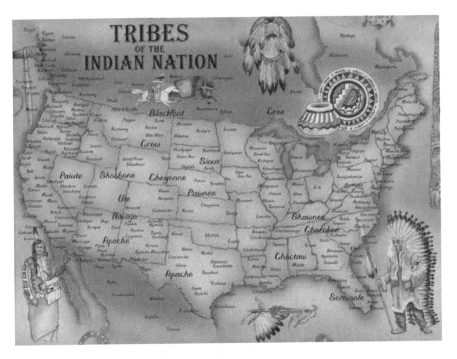

The Right to a Nationality

The right to a nationality is a fundamental human right. It implies the right of each individual to acquire, change and retain a nationality.

International human rights law provides that the right of States to decide who their nationals are is not absolute and, in particular, States must comply with their human rights obligations concerning the granting and loss of nationality.

Arbitrary Deprivation of Nationality

The right to retain a nationality corresponds to the prohibition of arbitrary deprivation of nationality. Arbitrary deprivation of nationality, therefore, effectively places the affected persons in a more disadvantaged situation concerning the enjoyment of their human rights because some of these rights may be subjected to lawful limitations that otherwise would not apply, but also because these persons are placed in a situation of increased vulnerability to human rights violations.

International Legal Framework

The right to a nationality is recognized in a series of international legal instruments, including the Universal Declaration of Human Rights, the International Convention on the Elimination of All Forms of Racial Discrimination, the International Covenant on Civil and Political Rights, the Convention on the Rights of the Child, the Convention on the Elimination of All Forms of Discrimination against Women, the Convention on the Nationality of Married Women, the Convention on the Rights of Persons with Disabilities and the International Convention on the Protection of the Rights of All Migrant Workers and Members of Their Families. The issue of nationality is also regulated in the Convention on the Reduction of Statelessness, the Convention relating to the Status of Stateless Persons and the Convention relating to the Status of Refugees.

An explicit and general prohibition of arbitrary deprivation of nationality can be found in numerous international instruments. In particular, it is worth noting that article 15 of the Universal Declaration of Human Rights explicitly provides that no one should be arbitrarily deprived of his or her nationality. The General Assembly, in its resolution 50/152, also recognized the fundamental nature of the prohibition of arbitrary deprivation of nationality.

Statelessness

The 1954 Convention relating to the Status of Stateless Persons defines "stateless person" as ï¿½a person who is not considered as a national by any State under the operation of its law.ï¿½ The exact number of stateless people is not known, but UNHCR estimates that there are at least 10 million globally. In addition to violations of their right to a nationality, stateless persons are subject to several other human rights violations. States shall introduce safeguards to prevent statelessness by granting their nationality to persons who would otherwise be stateless and are either born in their territory or are born abroad to one of their nationals.States shall also prevent statelessness upon loss or deprivation of nationality.

The Right to a Nationality and the Human Rights Council

The Human Right Council has addressed the enjoyment of the right to a nationality and the avoidance of statelessness in several resolutions on ï¿½Human rights and arbitrary deprivation of nationalityï¿½:

- Resolution 7/10 (2008)
- Resolution 10/13 (2009)
- Resolution 13/2 (2010)
- Resolution 20/4 on the Right to a Nationality: Women and Children (2012)
- Resolution 20/5 (2012)
- Resolution 26/14 (2014)

Work on the Right to a Nationality and on Statelessness

The People of all free national governments according to their national constitution are all of one [family] bearing one free national [name] title. Those who fail to recognize the free national [name] title of their constitutional government are classified as "undesirable," and are SUBJECT to all inferior NAMES and abuses and mistreatments that the People care to bestow upon them. And it is a sin for any group of people to violate the national constitutional laws of a free national government and cling to the NAMES and principles that deludes to slavery.

Prophet Noble Drew Ali

The Moors are the descendants of the ancient Moabites who inhabited the North Western and South Western shores of Africa.

- IMPORTANT INFORMATION -
NAME CORRECTION, PROCLAMATION AND JUDICIAL NOTICE
Before choosing your Free National Name it is important to make a few points to make your selection and sealing of your paperwork and receipt of your Nationality cards a seamless operation.

- Do not select a title, such as, King, Queen, Prince, Empress, Emperor, etc. as part of your Free National Name. This is called a "pre-title;" and there are no pre-titles in a Free National Name (appellation). For example, King Baylor Rahim Bey may be what you call yourself, but your actual paperwork should say Baylor Rahim Bey.

- Do not arbitrarily take the appellation "Ali" as part of your Free National Name. Although Moors often take this title, "Ali" is a title of Mastery, evidenced, among other things, by published scholarship.

- Do not select a Free National Name that includes multiple titles, i.e., Baylor Rahim El Bey or El Baylor Rahim Bey. In these examples, the Free National Name should be either Baylor Rahim El or Baylor Rahim Bey!

- When completing your paperwork, if the insertion sections are in "red" ink, make sure to change the ink color to "black" after making our inserts so the entire document's type is a continuous flow of the same ink color. In other words, do not send your paperwork in with both red and black ink in the body of the paperwork.

- When completing your paperwork, make sure your Free National Name is written in Upper and Lower case letters, while the STRAW NAME is written in ALL CAPS!

- Make sure to print your paperwork in color on 8 ½ x 14 inch (legal-sized) paper.

- When autographing (signing) your paperwork, you and your witnesses are to sign in "red" ink and complete the autograph with your right thumbprint in red.

- If family members and friends Nationalize and complete their paperwork at the same time, it is permissible to "witness" each other's paperwork in their Free National Names.

Mailing Locations to Send Name Declaration Correction and Publication and Judicial Notice and Proclamation

- Joseph Biden President of the United States Corporation Company 1600 Pennsylvania Avenue, NW. Washington, DC 20500.

- John Roberts [Chief Justice of the United States Supreme Court] 1 First Street North East, Washington, District of Columbia [20543]

- Steven T. Mnuchin The United States Department of the Treasury, Secretary of the Treasury, 1500 Pennsylvania Avenue, North West, Washington, District of Columbia [20220]

- Jeff Sessions Attorney General of the United States Department of Justice, 950 Pennsylvania Avenue, North West, Washington, District of Columbia [20530-0001]

- Mike Pompeo United States Secretary of State 2201 C Street, North West, Washington, District of Columbia [20530-0001]

- MG David P. Glaser PROVOST MARSHAL GENERAL OF THE UNITED STATES ARMY 2800 Army Pentagon, Washington, DC 20310-2800

- VIII. Archbishop near the TERRITORY you currently DOMICILE. A simple Google search will provide you with all Natural Persons to address the writs/affidavit.

- IX. Governor of the Corporate Territory you domicile near.

- X. [Antonio Guterres] SECRETARY OF THE UNITED NATIONS Care of 405 East Forty Second Street, New York, New York [10017] USA

Click the Link below for a Sample Nationality Affidavit

The Universal Declaration of Human Rights

The Universal Declaration of Human Rights (UDHR) is a milestone document in the history of human rights. Drafted by representatives with different legal and cultural backgrounds from all regions of the world, the Declaration was proclaimed by the United Nations General Assembly in Paris on 10 December 1948 (General Assembly resolution 217 A) as a common standard of achievements for all peoples and all nations. It sets out, for the first time, fundamental human rights to be universally protected and it has been translated into over 500 languages.

Download PDF

Preamble

Whereas recognition of the inherent dignity and of the equal and inalienable rights of all members of the human family is the foundation of freedom, justice and peace in the world,

Whereas disregard and contempt for human rights have resulted in barbarous acts which have outraged the conscience of mankind, and the advent of a world in which human beings shall enjoy freedom of speech and belief and freedom from fear and want has been proclaimed as the highest aspiration of the common people,

Whereas it is essential, if man is not to be compelled to have recourse, as a last resort, to rebellion against tyranny and oppression, that human rights should be protected by the rule of law,

Whereas it is essential to promote the development of friendly relations between nations,

Whereas the peoples of the United Nations have in the Charter reaffirmed their faith in fundamental human rights, in the dignity and worth of the human person and in the equal rights of men and women and have determined to promote social progress and better standards of life in larger freedom,

Whereas Member States have pledged themselves to achieve, in co-operation with the United Nations, the promotion of universal respect for and observance of human rights and fundamental freedoms,

Whereas a common understanding of these rights and freedoms is of the greatest importance for the full realization of this pledge,

Now, Therefore THE GENERAL ASSEMBLY proclaims THIS UNIVERSAL DECLARATION OF HUMAN RIGHTS as a common standard of achievement for all peoples and all nations, to the end that every individual and every organ of society, keeping this Declaration constantly in mind, shall strive by teaching and education to promote respect for these rights and freedoms and by progressive measures, national and international, to secure their universal and effective recognition and observance, both among the peoples of Member States themselves and among the peoples of territories under their jurisdiction.

Article 1.

All human beings are born free and equal in dignity and rights. They are endowed with reason and conscience and should act towards one another in a spirit of brotherhood.

Article 2.

Everyone is entitled to all the rights and freedoms set forth in this Declaration, without distinction of any kind, such as race, colour, sex, language, religion, political or other opinion, national or social origin, property, birth or other status. Furthermore, no distinction shall be made on the basis of the political, jurisdictional or international status of the country or territory to which a person belongs, whether it be independent, trust, non-self-governing or under any other limitation of sovereignty.

Article 3.

Everyone has the right to life, liberty and security of person.

Article 4.

No one shall be held in slavery or servitude; slavery and the slave trade shall be prohibited in all their forms.

Article 5.

No one shall be subjected to torture or to cruel, inhuman or degrading treatment or punishment.

Article 6.

Everyone has the right to recognition everywhere as a person before the law.

Article 7.

All are equal before the law and are entitled without any discrimination to equal protection of the law. All are entitled to equal protection against any discrimination in violation of this Declaration and against any incitement to such discrimination.

Article 8.

Everyone has the right to an effective remedy by the competent national tribunals for acts violating the fundamental rights granted him by the constitution or by law.

Article 9.

No one shall be subjected to arbitrary arrest, detention or exile.

Article 10.

Everyone is entitled in full equality to a fair and public hearing by an independent and impartial tribunal, in the determination of his rights and obligations and of any criminal charge against him.

Article 11.

(1) Everyone charged with a penal offence has the right to be presumed innocent until proved guilty according to law in a public trial at which he has had all the guarantees necessary for his defence.

(2) No one shall be held guilty of any penal offence on account of any act or omission which did not constitute a penal offence, under national or international law, at the time when it was committed. Nor shall a heavier penalty be imposed than the one that was applicable at the time the penal offence was committed.

Article 12.

No one shall be subjected to arbitrary interference with his privacy, family, home or correspondence, nor to attacks upon his honour and reputation. Everyone has the right to the protection of the law against such interference or attacks.

Article 13.

(1) Everyone has the right to freedom of movement and residence within the borders of each state.

(2) Everyone has the right to leave any country, including his own, and to return to his country.

Article 14.

(1) Everyone has the right to seek and to enjoy in other countries asylum from persecution.

(2) This right may not be invoked in the case of prosecutions genuinely arising from non-political crimes or from acts contrary to the purposes and principles of the United Nations.

Article 15.

(1) Everyone has the right to a nationality.

(2) No one shall be arbitrarily deprived of his nationality nor denied the right to change his nationality.

Article 16.

(1) Men and women of full age, without any limitation due to race, nationality or religion, have the right to marry and to found a family. They are entitled to equal rights as to marriage, during marriage and at its dissolution.

(2) Marriage shall be entered into only with the free and full consent of the intending spouses.

(3) The family is the natural and fundamental group unit of society and is entitled to protection by society and the State.

Article 17.

(1) Everyone has the right to own property alone as well as in association with others.
(2) No one shall be arbitrarily deprived of his property.

Article 18.

Everyone has the right to freedom of thought, conscience and religion; this right includes freedom to change his religion or belief, and freedom, either alone or in community with others and in public or private, to manifest his religion or belief in teaching, practice, worship and observance.

Article 19.

Everyone has the right to freedom of opinion and expression; this right includes freedom to hold opinions without interference and to seek, receive and impart information and ideas through any media and regardless of frontiers.

Article 20.

(1) Everyone has the right to freedom of peaceful assembly and association.
(2) No one may be compelled to belong to an association.

Article 21.

(1) Everyone has the right to take part in the government of his country, directly or through freely chosen representatives.
(2) Everyone has the right of equal access to public service in his country.
(3) The will of the people shall be the basis of the authority of government; this will shall be expressed in periodic and genuine elections which shall be by universal and equal suffrage and shall be held by secret vote or by equivalent free voting procedures.

Article 22.

Everyone, as a member of society, has the right to social security and is entitled to realization, through national effort and international co-operation and in accordance with the organization and resources of each State, of the economic, social and cultural rights indispensable for his dignity and the free development of his personality.

Article 23.

(1) Everyone has the right to work, to free choice of employment, to just and favourable conditions of work and to protection against unemployment.

(2) Everyone, without any discrimination, has the right to equal pay for equal work.

(3) Everyone who works has the right to just and favourable remuneration ensuring for himself and his family an existence worthy of human dignity, and supplemented, if necessary, by other means of social protection.

(4) Everyone has the right to form and to join trade unions for the protection of his interests.

Article 24.

Everyone has the right to rest and leisure, including reasonable limitation of working hours and periodic holidays with pay.

Article 25.

(1) Everyone has the right to a standard of living adequate for the health and well-being of himself and of his family, including food, clothing, housing and medical care and necessary social services, and the right to security in the event of unemployment, sickness, disability, widowhood, old age or other lack of livelihood in circumstances beyond his control.

(2) Motherhood and childhood are entitled to special care and assistance. All children, whether born in or out of wedlock, shall enjoy the same social protection.

Article 26.

(1) Everyone has the right to education. Education shall be free, at least in the elementary and fundamental stages. Elementary education shall be compulsory. Technical and professional education shall be made generally available and higher education shall be equally accessible to all on the basis of merit.

(2) Education shall be directed to the full development of the human personality and to the

strengthening of respect for human rights and fundamental freedoms. It shall promote understanding, tolerance and friendship among all nations, racial or religious groups, and shall further the activities of the United Nations for the maintenance of peace.

(3) Parents have a prior right to choose the kind of education that shall be given to their children.

Article 27.

(1) Everyone has the right freely to participate in the cultural life of the community, to enjoy the arts and to share in scientific advancement and its benefits.

(2) Everyone has the right to the protection of the moral and material interests resulting from any scientific, literary or artistic production of which he is the author.

Article 28.

Everyone is entitled to a social and international order in which the rights and freedoms set forth in this Declaration can be fully realized.

Article 29.

(1) Everyone has duties to the community in which alone the free and full development of his personality is possible.

(2) In the exercise of his rights and freedoms, everyone shall be subject only to such limitations as are determined by law solely for the purpose of securing due recognition and respect for the rights and freedoms of others and of meeting the just requirements of morality, public order and the general welfare in a democratic society.

(3) These rights and freedoms may in no case be exercised contrary to the purposes and principles of the United Nations.

Article 30.

Nothing in this Declaration may be interpreted as implying for any State, group or person any right to engage in any activity or to perform any act aimed at the destruction of any of the rights and freedoms set forth herein.

OVERVIEW

The right to a nationality is of paramount importance to the realization of other fundamental human rights. Possession of a nationality carries with it the diplomatic protection of the country of nationality and is also often a legal or practical requirement for the exercise of fundamental rights. Consequently, the right to a nationality has been described as the "right to have rights." *See* Trop v. Dulles, 356 U.S. 86, 101–02 (1958). Individuals who lack a nationality or an effective citizenship are therefore among the world's most vulnerable to human rights violations.

In recognition of the importance of having a nationality, a number of regional and international human rights instruments include the right to a nationality. **Article 15** of the Universal Declaration of Human Rights states that "[e]veryone has the right to a nationality" and that "[n]o one shall be arbitrarily deprived of his nationality nor denied the right to change his nationality." *See also* American Convention on Human Rights, **art. 20**. The right to a nationality is often articulated through protection of the rights of children and the principle of non-discrimination. For example, **Article 7** of the Convention on the Rights of the Child states that every child has the right to acquire a nationality, while **Article 5** of the Convention on the Elimination of All Forms of Racial Discrimination requires States to "prohibit and to eliminate racial discrimination in all its forms and to guarantee the right of everyone, without distinction as to race, colour, or national or ethnic origin, to equality before the law, notably in the enjoyment of the following rights . . . the right to nationality."

Despite recognition of the right to a nationality, there are currently at least **10 million people** who do not have a nationality and are therefore stateless. *See* UNHCR, Ending Statelessness. While statelessness is a global problem, it is particularly prevalent in South East Asia, Central Asia, Eastern Europe, the Middle East, and several countries in Africa. *See* UNHCR & Asylum Aid, *Mapping Statelessness in the United Kingdom* (2011), at 22. Estimates show that the countries with the greatest number of stateless persons residing within their borders are Cote d'Ivoire, Estonia, Kuwait, Latvia, Myanmar, Russia, Syria, Thailand, and Uzbekistan. *See* UNHCR, *Global Trends: Forced Displacement in 2016* (2017), at 60-63.

The 1954 Convention relating to the Status of Stateless Persons (1954 Statelessness Convention) was drafted in order to guarantee the protection of these individuals' fundamental rights. **Article 1(1)** of the 1954 Statelessness Convention defines a stateless person as **"a person who is not recognized as a national by any State under the operation of its law."** This definition has subsequently become a part of customary international law. *See* UNHCR, *Expert Meeting – The Concept of Stateless Persons Under International Law (Summary Conclusions)* (2010), at 2 (commonly referred to as the UNHCR Prato Summary Conclusions).

The 1954 Statelessness Convention is similar in structure to the 1951 Convention Relating to the Status of Refugees. This is because the 1954 Statelessness Convention was originally intended to be a Protocol to the 1951 Refugee Convention. *See, e.g.,* Equal Rights Trust, *The Protection of Stateless Persons in Detention under International Law* (Working Paper 2009), at 19. It is not surprising, therefore, that the

1954 Statelessness Convention addresses the same rights as those covered in the 1951 Refugee Convention, with a few distinctions. The 1954 Statelessness Convention applies some of the same exclusion clauses as those found in the 1951 Refugee Convention. For example, the 1954 Statelessness Convention does not apply "to persons who are at present receiving from organs or agencies of the United Nations other than the United Nations High Commissioner for Refugees protection or assistance so long as they are receiving such protection or assistance." *See* 1954 Statelessness Convention, art. 1(2)(i).

The 1954 Statelessness Convention also recognizes the **rights of stateless persons** to education, housing, access to the courts, employment, and public relief, among other rights. In some cases, such as in access to the courts and access to public relief and primary education, stateless persons are to be treated in the same way as nationals. *See id.* at arts. 16, 22-23. In other areas, including wage-earning employment and housing, stateless persons are to be given the same treatment as non-citizens in the same circumstances. *See id.* at arts. 17, 21. Recognizing that many stateless persons lack documentation, **Article 27** requires States to issue identity documents to stateless persons on their territory, while **Article 28** obliges States to issue travel documents to stateless persons unless there are compelling reasons such as national security or public order for not doing so. *See id.* at arts. 27-28.

A major limitation of the 1954 Statelessness Convention, and where it departs significantly from the 1951 Refugee Convention, is the protection afforded in **Article 31**. Article 31 prohibits the expulsion of stateless persons lawfully in the territory of a State party save for grounds of national security or public order. *See id.* at art. 31(1). **Article 31** also requires that the expulsion of stateless persons on these grounds be "in pursuance of a decision reached in accordance with due process of law." *See id.* at art. 31(2). The issue with **Article 31** is that it limits its protection to stateless persons *lawfully* on the State's territory. Because many stateless persons lack identity and travel documents, they have no means of gaining lawful entry into a State and thus are ineligible for protection from expulsion. This is in sharp contrast to Article 31 of the 1951 Refugee Convention, which recognizes the difficulties refugees often face in acquiring valid travel documents and prohibits States from penalizing refugees who enter their territories illegally. *See* 1951 Refugee Convention, art. 31(1).

Article 32 of the 1954 Statelessness Convention requires States to "as far as possible facilitate the assimilation and naturalization of stateless persons." More detailed provisions for the acquisition of nationality as well as the prevention of statelessness in the first place are found in the <u>1961 Convention on the Reduction of Statelessness</u> (1961 Statelessness Convention). **Article 1(2)** of the 1961 Statelessness Convention describes the conditions a State may place on granting nationality and stipulates that a State may require a period of habitual residence but it may not exceed five years. The 1961 Statelessness Convention also provides that children should acquire the nationality of the State in which they are born if they would otherwise be stateless and that a State may not deprive an individual of their nationality if doing so would render the individual stateless. *See* 1961 Statelessness Convention, arts. 1, 8.

Nationality can be a contentious issue, however, as the acquisition and deprivation of nationality implicates other areas of the law including a State's sovereign right to determine who may enter and remain within its territory. Consequently neither the 1954 nor the 1961 Statelessness Conventions are widely ratified and a large number of States have domestic laws that deprive individuals of access to a nationality on a discriminatory basis and/or do not adequately protect the human rights of stateless persons on their territory.

Legal Protections

The following instruments address the right to a nationality:

- 1951 Convention Relating to the Status of Refugees and 1967 Optional Protocol Relating to the Status of Refugees
- 1954 Convention Relating to the Status of Stateless Persons
- 1961 Convention on the Reduction of Statelessness
- 1997 European Convention on Nationality
- African Charter on the Rights and Welfare of the Child (art. 6)
- American Convention on Human Rights (art. 20)
- American Declaration of the Rights and Duties of Man (art. 19)
- Arab Charter on Human Rights (art. 24)
- Convention on the Elimination of All Forms of Discrimination against Women (art. 9)
- Convention on the Elimination of All Forms of Racial Discrimination (art. 5(d)(iii))
- Convention on the Rights of Persons with Disabilities (art. 18)
- Convention on the Rights of the Child (arts. 7 and 8)
- Council of Europe Convention on the Avoidance of Statelessness in Relation to State Succession
- International Covenant on Civil and Political Rights (art. 24(3))
- Protocol to the African Charter on Human and Peoples' Rights on the Rights of Women in Africa (Maputo Protocol) (art. 6(g) and (h))
- Universal Declaration of Human Rights (art. 15)

Acquisition of Nationality

Nationality can be acquired in one of three ways: by birth on a State's territory (*jus soli*), by descent from a State's national (*jus sanguinis*), or by naturalization. The citizenship laws of each State dictate whether the State applies *jus soli* or *jus sanguinis* and explain the requirements for naturalization. In States that apply pure *jus soli*, an individual acquires the citizenship of that State by being born on the State's territory, regardless of the citizenship or immigration status of the individual's parents. *See, e.g.*, 8 U.S.C. § 1401. In other States, such as the United Kingdom, an individual acquires citizenship by birth on the territory, provided that the individual's parents were "legally settled" in the United Kingdom at the time of the individual's birth. *See* British Nationality Act, 1981 c. 61, § 1 (United Kingdom). In States that apply *jus sanguinis*, it does not matter where an individual is born; if at least one of the individual's parents is a citizen of the country, citizenship will pass from the parent to the child. *See* Act of 15 February 1962 on Polish Citizenship, § 2 (Poland). A number of States, however, provide that only the father may pass his nationality on to his children. (See **Causes of Statelessness** below.) Finally, States such as the United States, apply both *jus soli* and *jus sanguinis* – that is, children born on U.S. territory are automatically U.S. citizens, as are children born abroad to U.S. citizen parents. *See* 8 U.S.C. § 1401.

De Jure vs. De Facto Statelessness

The definition of a stateless person provided in the 1954 Statelessness Convention – "a person who is not considered a national by any State under operation of its law" – describes the situation of the *de jure* stateless. *See* 1954 Statelessness Convention, art. 1(1). Thus, the obligations imposed on States by the 1954 Statelessness Convention apply only to *de jure* stateless persons, although the Final Act included a non-binding recommendation that States take measures to protect the rights of *de facto* stateless persons. *See* UN Conference of Plenipotentiaries on the Status of Refugees and Stateless Persons, *Final Act of the United Nations Conference of Plenipotentiaries on the Status of Refugees and Stateless Persons*, 25 July 1951, A/CONF.2/108/Rev.1.

There has been much debate within the international community concerning the definition of *de facto* statelessness. A generally applied definition of a *de facto* stateless person has been "a person unable to demonstrate that he/she is *de jure* stateless, yet he/she has no effective nationality and does not enjoy national protection." *See, e.g.,* Gábor Gyulai, Hungarian Helsinki Committee, *Forgotten Without Reason: Protection of Non-Refugee Stateless Persons in Central Europe* (2007), at 8. Thus, *de facto* stateless persons technically have a nationality, but for a variety of reasons do not enjoy the rights and protections that persons holding their nationality normally enjoy.

The debate regarding this definition has surrounded the ambiguity of the term "effective nationality." Traditionally, the divide has been over whether a person's nationality could be ineffective inside as well as outside the individual's country of nationality. This debate unfolded during the 2010 UNHCR Expert Meeting on the Concept of Statelessness under International Law, where participants ultimately concluded that the term "*de facto* statelessness" should refer to persons "outside the country of their nationality who are unable or, for valid reasons, are unwilling to avail themselves of the protection of that country." *See* UNHCR, *Expert Meeting – The Concept of Stateless Persons Under International Law (Summary Conclusions)* (2010), at 6.

In the above context, "protection" refers to "the right of diplomatic protection exercised by a State of nationality in order to remedy an internationally wrongful act against one of its nationals, as well as diplomatic and consular protection and assistance generally, including in relation to return to the State of nationality." *See id.* A person's inability or unwillingness to seek the protection of the country of that individual's nationality is often the result of a well-founded fear of persecution, meaning that refugees are considered *de facto* stateless. It is important to note, however, that not all *de facto* stateless persons are refugees. *See id.*

Causes of Statelessness

There are a variety of reasons why a person may be or become stateless. The most commonly discussed causes of statelessness are: State succession, conflict of laws and other technical or administrative matters, discrimination against certain racial or ethnic minority groups, and gender-based discrimination in nationality laws. *See, e.g.,* UNHCR & Asylum Aid, *Mapping Statelessness in the United Kingdom* (2011), at 23-24.

STATE SUCCESSION

The dissolution of the former Soviet Union and Yugoslav Federation as well as post-colonial State formation in Africa and Asia have contributed to large populations of stateless persons in Africa, Eastern Europe, and Asia. *See id* at 23. For example, when Estonia regained its independence in 1991, following over 40 years of Soviet occupation, the government restricted the automatic conferral of Estonian citizenship to persons who had been Estonian citizens prior to the Soviet occupation and their descendants. *See* Refugees International, *Left Behind: Stateless Russians Search for Equality in Estonia* (2004), at 1. As a result of this policy, "hundreds of thousands" of ethnic Russians living in Estonia – many of whom had been forcibly relocated to Estonia during the occupation – were left stateless. *See id.* Although the Estonian government has taken steps to encourage such individuals to apply for Estonian or Russian citizenship, the naturalization requirements for Estonian citizenship, such as the language requirement and civics exam, remain challenging for many ethnic Russians who live isolated from the ethnic Estonian population. *See id.*

The risk of statelessness in cases of State succession has led to the adoption of legal protections that specifically address nationality and State succession. **Article 10(1)** of the 1961 Statelessness Convention requires any treaty contracted between States concerning the transfer of territory to include specific provisions addressing the nationality of the citizens of the territory at issue. *See* 1961 Statelessness Convention, art. 10(1). In the absence of such provisions, a State is required to confer its nationality on residents of the transferred territory if they would otherwise become stateless. *See* 1961 Convention, art. 10(2). The Council of Europe has also drafted a <u>Convention on the Avoidance of Statelessness in Relation to State Succession</u>.

A future issue for the international community is the status of nationals of "sinking States" – that is, States that are in danger of physically disappearing as the result of climate change. This issue is without precedent and is currently being studied by relevant stakeholders within the international community. *See, e.g.*, Jane McAdam, *'Disappearing States', Statelessness and the Boundaries of International Law* (2010).

CONFLICT OF LAWS AND ADMINISTRATIVE PRACTICES

Statelessness cases in this context are the result of a variety of legal and administrative factors. The fact that some States apply *jus soli* while others apply *jus sanguinis* in their citizenship laws is one such factor. A person may be at risk of statelessness if she is born in a State that applies *jus sanguinis* while her parents were born in a State that applies *jus soli*, leaving the person ineligible for citizenship in both States due to conflicting laws. *See* UNHCR & Asylum Aid, *Mapping Statelessness in the United Kingdom*, at 23. Additionally, some States state in their nationality laws that a citizen will automatically lose their nationality after a specified period of absence from the State. *See id.* Because of the risk of statelessness these laws create, the 1961 Statelessness Convention provides that, with some limited exceptions, a person shall not be deprived of their nationality unless she has acquired or possesses another nationality. *See* 1961 Statelessness Convention, arts. 6-8.

Lack of registration at birth, which is a serious issue in developing countries, also places children at risk of statelessness. Although not having a birth certificate does not automatically make a child stateless, children who have no legal proof of where they were born, the identity of their parents, or the birthplace of their parents, are at a heightened risk of statelessness. UNHCR & Asylum Aid, *Mapping Statelessness in the United Kingdom*, at 23. The importance of birth registration can be seen in various international and regional human rights instruments that guarantee the right of every child to be registered at birth. *See* International Covenant on Civil and Political Rights, art. 24(2); Convention on the Rights of the Child, art. 7(1); African Charter on the Rights and Welfare of the Child, art. 6(2).

DISCRIMINATION AGAINST MINORITY GROUPS

In some cases, minority groups have either been prevented from acquiring the nationality of the country in which they reside or have been arbitrarily deprived of their nationality. A contemporary example of this problem can be seen in Sudan, where the government has been urged to ensure that Sudanese persons of southern origin are not stripped of their Sudanese citizenship if they do not become citizens of the new country of South Sudan. Similar concerns of statelessness have arisen in Burma, Syria, Iraq, and Kuwait in recent decades.

In 1982, the Rohingya, an ethnic minority group of Burma, were stripped of their Burmese citizenship. *See Refugees International, Bangladesh: The Silent Crisis* (2011). The Rohingya still residing in Burma have been consistently denied access to citizenship over the last several decades and have been subjected to violence as well as restrictions on their rights to marry and freedom of movement, among other severe human rights abuses. *See id.*

The Kurdish populations of Syria and Iraq have experienced a similar fate. In 1962, the Syrian government issued Decree No. 93 which announced a one-day census in the al-Hasakeh province, home to a large population of Syrian Kurds. *See* Human Rights Watch, *Syria: The Silenced Kurds* (1996). Residents were required to prove residence in Syria since 1945 or lose citizenship but residents were given insufficient notice of the census. *See id.* As a result, 120,000 Kurds were denaturalized, a figure accounting for 20 percent of Syria's Kurdish population at the time. *See id.* In 1980, Falil Kurds in Iraq were stripped of their citizenship following a decree issued by then-President Saddam Hussein. *See* UNHCR & Asylum Aid, *Mapping Statelessness in The United Kingdom*, at 24.

In other cases, certain ethnic groups within a country were deemed ineligible for citizenship following that country's acquisition of independence. In Kuwait, Article 1 of the 1959 Nationality Act states that any person or their descendants who settled in Kuwait prior to 1920 and maintained their residence there until enactment of the law is a Kuwaiti national. *See* Nationality Law, art. 1 (1959) (Kuwait). Through the application of this law, about one-third of Kuwait's population at the time of its independence was classified as Bidoon Jinsiya (without nationality). *See* Sebastian Kohn, *Stateless in Kuwait: Who Are the Bidoon?*, Open Society Foundations, 24 March 2011. It should be noted that some were in fact eligible for citizenship, but did not register during the relevant period because they misunderstood the importance of acquiring Kuwaiti citizenship. *See id.* Since the 1980s, the Bidoon in Kuwait have been treated, as illegal residents and have experienced discrimination in the employment and education sectors as well as in their ability to obtain legal documentation, including birth and marriage certificates. *See* Open Society Institute & Refugees International, *Without Citizenship: Statelessness, Discrimination and Repression in Kuwait* (20011), at 6-8. While the government has recently issued decrees allowing small numbers of Bidoon to naturalize, the majority of Bidoon remain stateless. *See id.*

Palestinians throughout the Middle East and North Africa have also been regularly denied access to citizenship. The 1965 Protocol for the Treatment of Palestinians in Arab States (Casablanca Protocol) provides that Arab States hosting Palestinian refugees are to treat them the same as citizens, while Palestinians "retain[] their Palestinian nationality." Consequently, Palestinians cannot attain nationality in many States in North Africa and the Middle East. *See* Laura van Waas, *The Situation of Stateless Persons in the Middle East and North Africa* (2010), at 42. The exception is Jordan, which granted citizenship to a large number of Palestinians through Article 3(2) of its Law No. 6 of 1954 on Nationality (last amended 1987). However, the Jordanian government has since restricted access to citizenship for Palestinians living within its borders. Between 2004 and 2008, the Jordanian government denaturalized more than 2,700 Jordanians of Palestinian origin and hundreds of thousands more were at risk of being denaturalized. *See* Human Rights Watch, *Stateless Again: Palestinian-Origin Jordanians Deprived of Their Nationality* (2010), at 1, 26.

Israel's nationality laws grant citizenship to Palestinians residing in Israel on the basis of residency within the State, though the International Crisis Group has reported that Arab-Israelis experience discrimination and marginalization. *See* Nationality Law, 5712-1952, (Israel); International Crisis Group, *Back to Basics: Israel's Arab Minority and the Israeli-Palestinian Conflict* (2012), at ii. In 2006, the controversial 2003 Nationality and Entry into Israel Law (Temporary Order), which, among other provisions, bars the Palestinian spouses of Israelis from access to citizenship and residency in Israel, was upheld by the High Court of Justice in 2006. *See High Court Rejects Petition against Citizenship Law*, Jerusalem Post, 11 January 2012.

Statelessness has had a profound effect on the lives of Palestinians. Unable to acquire citizenship and exercise the rights associated with it, many Palestinians live in poverty in refugee camps. The situation of Palestinians in Lebanon, where Lebanese law places serious restrictions on their ability to work and own property, is considered particularly dire. *See, e.g.*, Human Rights Watch, *World Report 2011: Lebanon* (2011). Meanwhile, the Palestinian populations of Kuwait and Libya were forcibly expelled in 1991 and 1995 respectively. *See, e.g.*, Abbas Shiblak, Stateless Palestinians, 26 Forced Migration Review 8 (2006).

GENDER-BASED DISCRIMINATION

In a large number of States that apply *jus sanguinis*, only men are able to pass their nationality on to their children. *See, e.g.*, Decree No. 15 on Lebanese Nationality, art. 1 (1925) (Lebanon). Although many of these States provide that children may acquire the nationality of their mother when the father is unknown or paternity has not been legally established, the children of citizen mothers and foreign fathers are at risk of statelessness if the father is stateless or is unwilling to complete the necessary steps to apply for citizenship for his child within the father's own country. *See, e.g.*, Nationality Law, art. 3 (1959) (Kuwait).

Article 9 of the Convention on the Elimination of All Forms of Discrimination against Women (CEDAW) recognizes the right of women to pass their nationality on to their children, as well as to their husbands. *See* CEDAW, art. 9. This provision has been weakened, however, by a significant number of States that have made reservations to this particular article. *See* UN Women, Declarations, Reservations and Objections to CEDAW (listing reservations to specific articles by country). Further, this right is restricted within Africa's regional human rights system. **Article 6(h)** of the Protocol to the African Charter on Human and Peoples' Rights on the Rights of the Women in Africa (Maputo Protocol) provides that women have equal rights with men to pass their nationality on to their children "except where this is contrary to a provision in national legislation or is contrary to national security interests." This is problematic because a number of countries in Africa have clauses in their national legislation that only permit men to pass their nationality on to their children. *See, e.g.,* Law No. 61-70 of 7 March 1961 Determining Senegalese Nationality, art. 5 (1961) (Senegal) (in French).

In recent years, some States have taken steps to grant women equal rights with respect to nationality. In 2011, Tunisia's interim government announced it was withdrawing all of its reservations to CEDAW, which included a reservation to Article 9. *See Tunisia: Government Lifts Restrictions on Women's Rights Treaty,* Human Rights Watch, 6 September 2011. In 2007, Morocco amended its nationality laws to enable women married to foreigners to pass their nationality on to their children. *See* Laura van Waas, *The Situation of Stateless Persons in the Middle East and North Africa* (2010), at 14. Egypt adopted similar measures in 2004 when it amended its Nationality Act to entitle children born to Egyptian mothers and foreign fathers to Egyptian citizenship. *See id.* at 13. However, in Egypt, women married to Palestinian men were still prevented from passing their nationality on to their children. *See id.* In May 2011, however, the Ministry of the Interior announced that these children would also be eligible for citizenship. *See* Women's Learning Partnership, *Women's Rights and the Arab Spring: Middle East/North Africa Overview and Fact Sheet.*

Consequences of Statelessness

Stateless persons live in an extremely precarious and vulnerable situation. Although humans have rights under international human rights law, individuals without citizenship lack the legal recognition necessary to exercise many rights, and have no expectation of diplomatic protection from any government. Statelessness affects a person's ability to enjoy fundamental privileges such as marriage, wage-earning employment, education, health, and freedom of movement. Consequently, "poverty becomes an integral part of stateless life." *See* UNHCR & Asylum Aid, *Mapping Statelessness in the United Kingdom,* at 25. Stateless persons are also particularly vulnerable to expulsion from their country of habitual residence because they lack a legal status and are at risk of prolonged detention, particularly in the context of pre-deportation detention, because there is often no State that will admit them. *See* Equal Rights Trust, The Protection of Stateless Persons in Detention under International Law (Working Paper, 2009), at 36–37.

ENFORCEMENT

Enforcement at the International Level

The United Nations High Commissioner for Refugees' (UNHCR) mandate holder has a duty to protect stateless persons, in addition to the duty to protect and assist refugees. *See* UNHCR, How UNHCR Helps Stateless People. This is in accordance with a series of General Assembly resolutions delegating the UNHCR as the UN body responsible for assisting stateless persons seeking benefits under the Statelessness

Conventions. *See* UN General Assembly, Resolution 3274 (XXIX), *Question of the establishment, in accordance with the Convention on the Reduction of Statelessness, of a body to which persons claiming the benefit of the Convention may apply*, UN Doc. A/RES/3274, 10 December 1974; UN General Assembly, Resolution 49/169, *Office of the United Nations High Commissioner for Refugees*, UN Doc. A/RES/49/169, 23 December 1994.

UNHCR's duties with regard to statelessness include identifying cases of statelessness, reducing statelessness, preventing statelessness, and providing assistance to stateless persons. *See id.* During the 50th anniversary year of the 1961 Statelessness Convention, the UNHCR led a campaign to increase the protection of stateless persons by encouraging more countries to ratify the two Statelessness Conventions and by holding a series of expert meetings on their key provisions. As a result of UNHCR's efforts, 17 more countries acceded to the 1954 Statelessness Convention and/or the 1961 Statelessness Convention between 2011 and 2012. *See* UNHCR, UN Conventions on Statelessness. The UNHCR also drew from the summary conclusions of its expert meetings to draft a series of guidelines on issues such as the definition of statelessness in Article 1(1) of the 1954 Statelessness Convention, statelessness identification procedures, and the status of stateless persons at the national level.

Enforcement at the National Level

The 1954 Statelessness Convention does not include procedures for States to use in identifying stateless persons on their territory. Thus, in addition to the low number of States that have ratified the Statelessness Conventions, a major factor limiting protection of stateless persons at the national level is the general lack of statelessness identification procedures. *See, e.g.,* UNHCR & Asylum Aid, *Mapping Statelessness in the United Kingdom*, at 64. Statelessness identification procedures are necessary because only once an individual has been recognized as being stateless is he or she entitled to the protections of the 1954 Statelessness Convention and the relevant national legislation incorporating those protections. In the absence of statelessness status determination procedures, many stateless individuals apply for asylum in an attempt to access some form of legal protection. *See id.* at 39. This is problematic, as many stateless persons do not have a well-founded fear of persecution and consequently do not qualify as refugees. Ineligible for protection as refugees and without access to recognition as a stateless person, these individuals often find themselves in legal limbo. *See id.* at 59.

A lack of statelessness determination procedures does not necessarily mean a lack of protection for stateless persons, however. Some States without formal statelessness determination procedures offer stateless persons a form of subsidiary protection. *See, e.g.,* Gábor Gyulai, Hungarian Helsinki Committee, *Forgotten Without Reason: Protection of Non-Refugee Stateless Persons in Central Europe*, at 3. This generally consists of a renewable residence permit and travel documents. *See id.* at 24,

40. Persons who qualify for subsidiary protection may also have access to education, employment, and social services, although such access is often subject to the same restrictions that are applied to foreign nationals within the State's territory and in some cases amounts to a lesser form of protection than that granted to refugees. *See id.* at 25.

Some States, even those not party to the 1961 Statelessness Convention, have implemented national measures to reducing statelessness. A large number of States consider abandoned children found within their territory to be nationals absent evidence to the contrary. *See, e.g.,* Law of 15 February 1962 on Polish Citizenship, art. 5 (1962) (Poland). Some States provide access to nationality to children born on their territory to stateless parents. *See, e.g., id.* A number of States also provide more lenient naturalization requirements for stateless persons. For example, Hungary reduces its continuous residence requirement from eight years to five years for stateless persons. *See* Gábor Gyulai, Hungarian Helsinki Committee, *Forgotten Without Reason: Protection of Non-Refugee Stateless Persons in Central Europe*, at 30.

SELECTED CASELAW

Access to Nationality

- The European Convention on Human Rights does not address the right to a nationality. Nonetheless, the European Court of Human Rights (ECtHR) has recognized that in some cases, lack of access to a nationality or the removal of stateless persons from a nation may infringe on an individual's right to respect for his/her private or family life as recognized in Article 8 of the European Convention. In Kurić and Others v. Slovenia, citizens of the Socialist Federal Republic of Yugoslavia were "erased" from Slovenia's registry of permanent residents and rendered stateless when Slovenia gained its independence and they failed to register as permanent residents or citizens during a prescribed period. *See* ECtHR, *Kurić and Others v. Slovenia* [GC], no. 26828/06, Judgment of 26 June 2012, paras. 31–33. The Court held that Slovenia violated the applicants' rights under Article 8 because the registration procedures were arbitrary and unlawful, and the purpose of registering – particularly when the applicants were already included in a registry of permanent residents – was not adequately explained. *See id.* at paras. 360-62; *cf.* ECtHR, *Karassev and Family v. Finland* (dec.), no. 31414/96, ECHR 1999-II, Judgment of 12 January 1999 (acknowledging the Article 8 right, but finding the case inadmissible where Finland's determination that the applicant was a Russian citizen was based on a legitimate interpretation of Russian law, despite conflicting reports on his citizenship from the Russian consulate, and where the applicant and his family were eligible for Finnish residency and under no risk of deportation).

- The African Charter on the Rights and Welfare of the Child (African Children's Charter) does explicitly recognize the right to a nationality. *See* African Children's Charter, art. 6. In one case, the African Committee of Experts on the Rights and Welfare of the Child (ACERWC) found that Kenya had violated the rights of children of Nubian descent under the African Children's Charter. *See* ACERWC, *Institute for Human Rights and*

Development in Africa and the Open Society Justice Initiative (on Behalf of Children of Nubian Descent in Kenya) v. Kenya, Communication No. 002/Com/002/2009, Judgment of 22 March 2011, para. 69. Many children of Nubian descent in Kenya had been left stateless when they were neither registered nor given access to Kenyan citizenship upon being born in Kenya, thus violating their right to a nationality. *See id.* at paras. 4, 40, 69. The Committee also found that the rigorous vetting process Nubian children were required to undergo to obtain identity documents amounted to discriminatory treatment for which there was no justification. *See id.* at paras. 43, 55-56. Finally, the Committee held that the consequences of statelessness, namely limited access to education, employment, and health services, also constituted a violation of the children's rights under the African Children's Charter. *See id.* at paras. 61-62.

Detention and Removal of Stateless Persons

- In <u>Al-Kateb v. Godwin</u>, the High Court of Australia upheld the indefinite detention of a stateless Palestinian from Kuwait. *See Al-Kateb v. Godwin* [2004] HCA 37, paras. 74–75 (Australia). The High Court held that indefinite detention of an unlawful non-citizen subject to removal from Australia was permitted under the Migration Act and that such detention did not violate Article III of the Australian Constitution. *See id.* The decision was met with strong criticism and resulted in the issuance of Bridging Visas to individuals who, like Al-Kateb, have no country willing to accept them. *See* Equal Rights Trust, *The Protection of Stateless Persons in Detention under International Law* (Working Paper, 2009), at 38.

- The U.S. Supreme Court, by contrast, has taken a different approach. In *Zadvydas v. Davis*, the Supreme Court held that in order to hold a non-citizen in detention pending removal beyond six months, the United States must show removal is likely in the foreseeable future or special circumstances warrant continued detention. *See* Zadvydas v. Davis, 533 U.S. 678, 701–02 (2001). *Zadvydas*concerned two former permanent residents unable to be returned to their country of origin – Zadvydas who was of Lithuanian descent but was *de jure* stateless and Kim who was a Cambodian national but whom the Cambodian government refused to re-admit. *See id.* at 784–86. The Supreme Court later held in *Clark v. Martinez* that the reasonable time limit also applied to inadmissible aliens. *See* Clark v. Martinez, 543 U.S. 371, 386 (2005).

- In *Kelzani v. Secretary of State for the Home Department*, the Immigration Appellate Authority of the United Kingdom held that the deportation of Kelzani, a stateless Palestinian who had violated the terms of his visa by engaging in unauthorized employment and subsequently overstayed his visa, did not violate Article 31 of the 1954 Statelessness Convention because "the control of immigration is necessary for maintenance of the public order" and his deportation order had been issued in accordance with the principles of due process. *See Kelzani v. Secretary of State for the Home Department*, [1978] Imm AR 193 (United Kingdom); UNHCR & Asylum Access, *Mapping Statelessness in the United Kingdom*, at 67. The tribunal also held that it was irrelevant that the travel document that had been issued to Kelzani by the Egyptian government did not entitle Kelzani to permanent residence in Egypt, as there was evidence that he would be admitted to Egypt and have access to employment there. *See id.* The case has been widely criticized and some speculate that if a similar case were to be brought today it would come out differently. *See* UNHCR & Asylum Aid, *Mapping Statelessness in the United Kingdom*, at 67.

Arbitrary Deprivation of Nationality

- In 2005, the Inter-American Court of Human Rights held that the Dominican Republic violated multiple articles of the <u>American Convention on Human Rights</u> when it refused to issue birth certificates to children born in the Dominican Republic to parents of Haitian descent. *See* I/A Court H.R., *Girls Yean and Bosico v. Dominican Republic.* Preliminary Objections, Merits, Reparations and Costs. Judgment of September 8, 2005, Series C No. 130, para. 260. The Inter-American Court held that the Dominican Republic's interpretation of "in transit" in its migration and citizenship laws excluded ethnic Haitians born in the Dominican Republic from acquiring citizenship and that its treatment of ethnic Haitians in the Dominican Republic was arbitrary and discriminatory. *See id.* at para. 174. The Inter-American Court also found a violation of the children's right to education, since the girls were unable to attend school as a result of not being issued birth certificates. *See id.* at paras. 185–87.

- In *John K. Modise v. Botswana*, the African Commission on Human and Peoples' Rights held that Modise was a citizen of Botswana by birth, as he had been born in South Africa to a father who was a British Protected Person and was therefore considered a citizen of Botswana following its independence. *See* ACommHPR, *John K. Modise v. Botswana*, Communication No. 97/93, Merits Decision, 28th Ordinary Session, 6 November 2000, para. 97. The Commission held that Botswana had violated Modise's rights under the African Charter on Human and Peoples' Rights by not recognizing him as a citizen and by deporting him from Botswana, which resulted in his living in poverty. *See id.* at para. 92. The Commission held that Modise's living conditions while he was stateless amounted to a violation of his right to respect for dignity. *See id.* The Commission further noted that Botswana's grant of registered citizenship to Modise was inadequate because registered citizens did not have the same rights as citizens by birth. *See id.* at paras. 83, 96–97.

Equal Access to Nationality

- In an advisory opinion, the Inter-American Court of Human Rights found that the proposed constitutional amendments granting preferential naturalization requirements to women married to Costa Rican men but not to men married to Costa Rican women would amount to discrimination under the American Convention on Human Rights. *See* I/A Court H.R., *Proposed Amendments to the Naturalization Provision of the Constitution of Costa Rica,* Advisory Opinion OC-4/84, 19 January 1984, paras. 64–67. The Court also held that the provisions giving preferential treatment to non-citizens from Central American or other Spanish-speaking cultures did not amount to discrimination. *See id.* at paras. 60–61, 68. A proposed revision requiring foreign women who lost their nationality upon marriage to a Costa Rican man to wait two years before they could acquire Costa Rican nationality did not violate the right to a nationality under Article 20 of the Convention because it did not amount to an arbitrary deprivation of nationality on the part of Costa Rica, but the Court cautioned that some of the women affected by the provision could be left stateless during the two-year period. *See id.* at paras. 46, 48, 68.

- At the domestic level, the Court of Appeal of Botswana held that the Citizenship Act of 1984, which granted citizenship to the children of a Botswanan father and to children born out of wedlock to a Botswanan mother, violated the Constitutional guarantees of freedom from discrimination and freedom of movement and liberty since the children of the plaintiff, a Botswanan woman married to a foreign national, could face removal from Botswana as non-citizens and because the law discouraged marriage between citizen women and non-citizen men. *See Attorney-General v. Dow* (2001) AHRLR 99 (BwCA 1992), paras. 124, 130, 134.

STATUTES/ACTS	THE LAW
The **LEGISLATURE** makes Statutes by the en-Act-ments of Legislation	The **PEOPLE** make The Law by the acceptance/validation of Jury decisions
"Statutes" are **"Legal Contracts"**, prescribed as "Acts/Bills/Legislative Instruments"	"The Law" is the People's **"Common Law"**, recorded in real time as "Case Law"
Acts are offered **CONTRACTS** made effective by the informed **CONSENT** of a Man/Woman	Laws are moral **CUSTOMS** made effective by the **CONSCIENCE** of the People
'**ACT**, civil law, contracts. A writing which states in a legal form that a thing has been said, done, or agreed.' [Bouvier's Law Dictionary, 1856 Edition]	'**LAW.** When considered in relation to its origin, i is statute law or common law.' [Bouvier's Law Dictionary, 1856 Edition]
'**STATUTE.** The written will of the legislature...; an <u>act</u> of the legislature. ... This word is used in contradistinction to the common law. ... It is a general rule that when the provision of a statute is general, everything which is necessary to make such provision effectual is supplied by the common law.' [Bouvier's Law Dictionary, 1856 Edition]	'**LAW.** As a compound adjective "common-law" i: understood as contrasted with or opposed t("statutory." ' [Black's Law Dictionary, 2nd Edition]
STATUTES GOVERN LEGAL ENTITIES as a franchise benefit to the State	**THE LAW PROTECTS THE PEOPLE** from harm, loss, and deceit
We are **NOT ALL EQUAL** in the texts of Statutes	We are **ALL EQUAL** in the eyes of The Law
Statutes are based on **PRACTICALITIES**	Laws are based on **PRINCIPLES**
Statutes can **QUICKLY** come and go	Laws evolve over **TIME** and often endure
LEGAL refers to **LEGISLATION**	**LAWFUL** refers to **THE LAW**
The Legislature cannot overturn Case Law	A Jury of People can overturn a Statute
Statutes can serve The Law but cannot diminish or expand The Law	Laws can be taken into Statutes but if repealed in Statute they remain in Law
"Non-Positive Law" - Statute <u>not</u> serving The Law	"Positive Law" - Statute serving The Law
"Colour of Law" - Misuse of authority without right	"Moral Law" - Principle of right living
De facto "in practice"	**De jure** "in law"
Admiralty Maritime Commercial **"Law of the Sea"**	The People's Common Law **"Law of the Land"**
PROFIT and **DISPUTE**	**PEOPLE** and **PEACE**
STATUTES are **ARTIFICIAL**	**THE LAW** is **LIVING**

2. <u>Status correction</u>

"NAME"	"Appellation"
noun, verb, plural noun	*noun, proper noun*
of Law: *Nomen est quasi rei notamen.* ame is, as it were, the distinctive sign (or signifier) of a **thing**.	1. The definition of an appellation is the name of someone. (An example of an a, is the name Tom.) [Webster's Dictionary
"JOHN HENRY DOE"	**"John-Henry"**
Legally "registered" Vessel	Lawfully "recorded" Estate
Law of the Sea	**Law of the Land**
Admiralty Maritime Jurisdiction	Common Law Jurisdiction

WHAT IS STATUS?

THE STATUS OF A PERSON IS HIS OR HERS LEGAL POSITION OR CONDITION.

CERTAIN RIGHTS AND DUTIES WITH CERTAIN CAPACITY AND INCAPACITY OR A CERTAIN CLASS FOR A CERTAIN PERSON CONSTITUE A CERTAIN CONDITION OR STATUS

SO STATUS PRONOUNCES WHAT YOU ACTUALLY HAVE THE RIGHTS FOR

A CITIZEN IS NOT A PERSON ENTITLED TO CONSTITUTIONAL PER STATUS IN COURT

YOUR STATUS IS ONE THING AND HOW COURT PERCEIVES STATUS IS ANOTHER ON HOW THE LAW APPLIES TO YOU. SO YOU SHOULD UPDATE YOUR STATUS AS A NATIONAL AND NOT A FEDERAL CITIZEN.

SO ONCE YOU KNOW WHO YOU ARE AND HOW THEY APPLY TO YOU THEN YOU KNOW HOW TO INVOKE YOUR RIGHTS PROPERLY.

SOME EXAMPLES ARE CITIZEN

US CITIZEN RESIDENT

STATE CITIZEN

AMERICAN NATIONAL

NON – RESIDENT

FOREIGN NATIONAL

FOREIGN RESIDENT

TOURIST

SECURED CREDITOR

SINGLE

MARRIED ETC

YOUR STATUS IS CRITICAL OF HOW YOU WILL BE TREATED UNDER LAW

WHAT IS STANDING?

PROPER STANDING TO PRESENT ITSELF TO COURT

STANDING HAS REQUIREMENTS

INJURY IN FACT MUST HAVE SUFFERED OR WILL SUFFER

CAUSEATION CONNECTION BETWEEN THE INJURY AND TH CONDUCT COMPLAINED OF AND NOT RESULT OF SOME THIRD PARTY IN FRONT OF THE COURT

REDRESSABILITY IT MUST BE LIKELY AS OPPOSED TO SPECULATIVE. THE COURT CAN RESOLVE THE MATTER PROPERLY

EXAMPLES

PLANTIFF

DEFANDANTS

ATTORNEYS

CALLED WITNESSES

FRIENDS OF THE COURT

A RIGHT OF PEOPLE TO CHALLENGE THE CONDUCT OF ANOTHER IN A COURT

AGENCY AND ATTORNEY AKA AGENTS MEAN SAMETHING AND ACT ONLY ON BEHALF OF A CORPORATION FUCTIONARY OF THE CORPORATE WORLD ANY CORPORATION NEEDS AN AGENT AND ANYWHERE THERE IS AN AGENT THERE IS A PRINCIPLE SO THERE HAS TO BE A REGISTERED OFFICE AND A REGISTERED AGENT TO RECEIVE SERVICE OF PROCESS

YOU ARE PRESUMMED TO BE THE DEAD ENTITY ACTIN IN CAPACITY FOR THE PRINCIPLE FOR ALL CAPS STRAWMAN NAME ITS THIS AGENCY RELATIONSHIP THAT MAKES YOU LIABLE TO PAY THE LEVY AND CHARGES PLACED UPON THIS DEAD ENITITY

SO TO GET OUT THIS SITUATION YOU MUST SERVE TIES OR TAKE OWNERSHIP OF THE ESTATE

ATTORN MEANS TO TURN OVER MONEY RENT OT FOODS TO ANTOTHER

ATTORNEY IS AN AGENT OR SOMETHING AUTHORIZED TO ACT FOR ANOTHER

ATTORNEY IN FACT ALTERNATE A LEGAL APPOINTEED LEGAL REP PROXY OR SURROGATE

POWER OF ATTORNEY THE PRINCIPLE APPOINTS ANOTHER PERSON TO ACT AS AN AGENT OR IT CAN BE LIMITED TO CERTAIN FUNCTIONS TERMS AND CONDITIONS PRINCIPLE CAN REVOKE POWER OF ATTORNEY AT ANY TIME

ATTORNEY OF LAW MEANS COLOR OF LAW OF MEANS WITHOUT COLOR MEANS FICTION OR SIMILAR TO SOMETHING THAT IS REAL

LAW OF THE FLAG AND OR CORPOATE SEAL OR STAMP

A PRINCIPLE OF MARITIME AND INTERNATION LAW THAT THE SAILORS AND THE VESSEL WILL BE SUBJECT TO THE LAWS OF THE STATE CORESPONDING TO THE FLAG FLOWN BY THE VESSEL

DECLARATION
OF STATUS
:Could-Be: Anyone
Private American Free Man

I, First-Middle of the family Last, a creation of the Supreme Creator (God), in *esse* and *sui juris*, have reached the age of majority, am of sound mind and competent to testify, do hereby declare the following truths to the best of my knowledge and belief:

1. Declarant is the Divine Spirit incarnate as man. There is no proof to the contrary;

2. Declarant was born alive on the geographic location body known as Birth State. There is no proof to the contrary;

3. Declarant's given name is First-Middle and his family name is Last. Exhibit A annexed hereto and made a part hereof. There is no proof to the contrary;

4. Declarant does not consent to being a U.S. Citizen nor any citizen of any corporate body politic on Earth and as such is alien to the jurisdiction of the United States. There is no proof to the contrary;

5. Declarant is always in Peace and Honor as an American National whereas Declarant is not an enemy, belligerent, rebel or terrorist subject to the Trading with The Enemy Act of October 6, 1917, the Emergency Banking Relief Act of March 9, 1933, the Patriot Act of October 26, 2001 or any other public policy and/or statute of the United States or its subsidiary States, possessions or territory. There is no proof to the contrary;

6. Declarant does not consent to any express or implied contracts, trust indentures, trust instruments, bailment agreements and/or any agreements made either publicly or privately with any natural or artificial person and hereby terminates all agreements on the grounds they were previously signed by Declarant under threat, duress, incompetence or without full disclosure wherefore Declarant hereby declares all said contracts null and void *nunc pro tunc ab initio*. There is no proof to the contrary;

7. Declarant does not reside on any Federal land lawfully ceded to the United States of America, the United States or any territory possession thereof. There is no proof to the contrary;

8. Declarant is NOT property of, surety for or joined with FIRST MIDDLE LAST; First Middle Last; LAST, FIRST MIDDLE; Last, First Middle; First LAST; LAST, First; or any derivation of that name either in spelling or capitis and when in public goes only by the name First-Middle of the family Last. There is no proof to the contrary;

9.   Declarant acknowledges and accepts the Uniform Commercial Code definition of "registered organization" in Article 9-102(a)(71) as "means an organization organized solely under the law of a single State or the United States by the filing of a public organic record with, the issuance of a public organic record by, or the enactment of legislation by the State or the United States." There is no proof to the contrary;

10.   Declarant acknowledges and accepts the Uniform Commercial Code definition of "goods" in Article 9-102(a)(44)(iii) as "the unborn young of animals." There is no proof to the contrary;

11.   Declarant acknowledges and accepts the Black's Law 7th Ed. dictionary definition of "best evidence" as "evidence of the highest quality available, as measured by the nature of the case rather than the thing offered as evidence... See BEST-EVIDENCE RULE." There is no proof to the contrary;

12.   Declarant as Grantee acknowledges and accepts all interest, rights and title to the registered organization FIRST MIDDLE LAST identified by the Your State Health Division Vital Records Unit Certificate of Live Birth state file No.: 123-45-678910 registered and filed in City, State, including all its accounts, instruments, goods and property et. al. including social security account number ending in xxx-xx-1234 from the Grantor United States of America. Exhibit B annexed hereto and made a part hereof. The original certified copy of the Certificate of Live Birth (true and correct copy on page Exhibit B page 5 of 5) has a 9-digit number number on the back ending in xxxx12345 and can also be used to help identify the registered organization FIRST MIDDLE LAST. There is no proof to the contrary;

13.   Declarant believes that the registered organization FIRST MIDDLE LAST may also be identified by the State Department of Human Resources Vital Records Unit Certificate of Live Birth state file No.: 123-45-678910, the Your State Health Authority Public Health Division Vital Records Unit Certificate of Live Birth state file No.: 123-45-678910, the Certificate of Live Birth state file No.: 123-45-678910 held by the Your State Vital Records Agency, the true and correct copy of the original certificate on file, and/or the vital records facts on file with the Your Stste Center for Health Statistics. There is no proof to the contrary;

14.   Declarant believes that the registered organization FIRST MIDDLE LAST may also be identified by the document/certificate originally and officially registered/filed (local file No.: 12345) by County Registrar's Name, the Your County Registrar at the time of birth, at/with the Office of the Your County Registrar on COLB Birth Date, and that the registered organization FIRST MIDDLE LAST may also be identified by the true and exact reproduction of the official registered/filed document/certificate, issued to Declarant's father and mother, by Your County, as a Certification of Vital Record, on COLB Registration Date. Exhibit C annexed hereto and made a part hereof. The true and exact reproduction of the original document registered/filed (true and correct copy on page 2 of 2 of Exhibit C) has a 6-digit number on the back/front ending in xxx123 and can also be used to help identify the registered organization FIRST MIDDLE LAST. There is no proof to the contrary;

15. Declarant is not surety for any registered organization or artificial entity *nunc pro tunc ab initio*. Exhibit D annexed hereto and made a part hereof. There is no proof to the contrary;

16. Declarant hereby resigns all assumed, presumed, or express agency with any legal fiction public and private corporate bodies, governments, associations et. al. Exhibit E annexed hereto and made a part hereof. There is no proof to the contrary;

17. Declarant hereby appoints :Could-Be: Anyone to the position of General Executor for the FIRST MIDDLE LAST, Estate. Exhibit F annexed hereto and made a part hereof. There is no proof to the contrary;

Further Declarant sayeth naught.

I, First-Middle of the family Last, affirm under penalty of perjury, under the laws of the United States of America, that the foregoing is true and correct to the best of my knowledge and belief so help me God. [28 USC 1746(1)]

Executed this_____day of_____two thousand nineteen.

Without Prejudice

:Could-Be: Anyone
Private American Free Man, Yourstateian
c/o Post Road: Address
City, State Spelled Out no ZIP

DECLARATION OF PROPER NAME

I, First-Middle of the family Last, a creation of the Supreme Creator (God), in *esse* and *sui juris*, solemnly affirm and declare that I was naturally born on the DATE of Actual birth day of Month in the Year Nineteen Hundred Ninety-Five (March 5, 1995). On that day. My natural and legal parents, First-Middle of the family Last and First-Middle of the family Last (nee Maiden), gave me the name of "First-Middle". Inheriting the family name of "Last", I am ":Could-Be: Anyone", the name correctly spelled with both upper and lower case letters according to the English rules of grammar pertaining to the spelling of a proper name and surname/family name of an individual natural person.

I, :Could-Be: Anyone, am neither a member of the United States Armed Forces, nor am I a rebel, belligerent, enemy or terrorist publicly residing in an occupied territory under rule of martial conqueror/commander in chief. Therefore, I am not "FIRST MIDDLE LAST, First Middle Last; LAST, FIRST MIDDLE; Last, First Middle" or any derivation of said name of war/*nom de guerre*.

I am :Could-Be: Anyone.

> Maxim: *"Equity regards as done that which ought to have been done."*

I, First-Middle of the family Last, affirm under penalty of perjury, under the laws of the United States of America, that the foregoing is true and correct to the best of my knowledge and belief so help me God. [28 USC 1746(1)]

Executed this_____day of_____two thousand nineteen.

Without Prejudice

:Could-Be: Anyone
Private American Free Man, Yourstateian
c/o Post Road: Address
City, State Spelled Out no ZIP

<u>DECLARATION DISCLAIMER OF TRUSTEESHIP RESIGNATION OF REGISTERED AGENT</u>

I, First-Middle of the family Last, a creation of the Supreme Creator (God), in *esse* and *sui juris*, have reached the age of majority, am of sound mind and competent to testify, do hereby declare the following truths to be the best of my knowledge and belief:

1. Declarant hereby resigns resident agency and disclaims any and all trusteeship, express and/or implied, public and/or private, knowingly or unknowingly provided by Declarant on behalf of the State of Oregon registered organization "FIRST MIDDLE LAST", including any and all derivations and capitis of that name, on file with the Office of the Your County Name County Registrar and Your State Vital Records unit state file No.: 123-45-678910 and local file No.: 12345, created by the filing of an organic public record on Date of Birth registration not DOB;

2. Declarant hereby resigns resident agency and extends this disclaimer to every public and/or private government trust relation be it federal, state, county and/or city. This disclaimer and refusal of trusteeship and resignation of resident agent includes, but is not limited to, permits, licenses including driver's licenses, business and marriage licenses, social security card agreements, voter's registration, birth certificates, insurance applications, federal student loans, student aid and all other student documentation, taxpayer identification numbers, marriage, warrants, any and all court documents civil or criminal, bonds, commercial paper, traffic tickets, selective service applications for military, passports, any and all government ID, and every paper presumed to be a contract or not, ever signed by Declarant with another party having a legal person identity, be they public or private, and every public government trust relation, known or unknown, evidencing an express or implied trusteeship on behalf of the State of Oregon, registered organization/Public U.S. citizen "FIRST MIDDLE LAST", including any and all derivations and capitis' of that name, on file with the Office of the Your County Name County Registrar and Your State Vital Records unit state file No.: 123-45-678910 and local file No.: 12345, originally filed by Name of County Register if known, County Registrar for Your Birth County Name, Birth State;

This disclaimer concerning registered organization/U.S. citizen person "FIRST MIDDLE LAST" Office of the Your County Name County Registrar and Your State Vital Records unit state file No.: 123-45-678910 and local file No.: 12345, is retroactive *nunc pro tunc ab initio* to the date of COLB REGISTRATION DATE NOT DOB, which is the date of creation of the registered organization.

Maxim: "Equity regards as done that which ought to have been done."

Further Declarant Sayeth Naught.

I, First-Middle of the family Last, affirm under penalty of perjury, under the laws of the United States of America, that the foregoing is true and correct to the best of my knowledge and belief so help me God. [28 USC 1746(1)]

Executed this_____day of_____two thousand nineteen.

Without Prejudice

BY ....A.R....

RECESSION OF SURETY

I, First-Middle of the family Last, a creation of the Supreme Creator (God), in *esse* and *sui juris*, have reached the age of majority, am of sound mind and competent to testify, do hereby affirm the following truths to be the best of my knowledge and belief:

1. Declarant hereby rescinds and revokes, *nunc pro tunc ab initio* every signature of suretyship, public and private, ever provided by Declarant on behalf of the registered organization, U.S. citizen "FIRST MIDDLE LAST"

created by the filing of an organic public record on Date Filed w/registrar on COLB *nunc pro tunc ab initio*. There is no proof to the contrary;

2.   Declarant extends this rescission of surety to every public entity and government contract be it federal, state, county, and/or city (including the CITY OF CHICAGO, a Municipal Corporation), including but not limited to, the initial application for a social security number/taxpayer identification number; every individual and/or corporate tax return ever filed be it federal, state, county and/or city; every application for a business license and business license number; every court document ever signed in any legal action, civil and/or criminal; every contract and court document signed as a defendant or probationer; the initial application for selective service in the Armed Forces of the United States; every adhesion contract and application for an individual driver's license and learner's permit; every application for an individual state identification card, including ID. No.: 1234-5678-910B; every application for a United States passport, including the application for passport No.: 123456789 and passport card No.: C12345678, every application for voter registration as well as every voter registration card, including the application forwarded to CHICAGO BOARD OF ELECTIONS, Application No.: B123-4567-8910 3032013101100425065; and every other public government contract, known and unknown, evidencing a signature of suretyship, every signature now being a signature of agency without recourse/without prejudice by the sole beneficiary, *nunc pro tunc ab initio*. There is no proof to the contrary;

3.   Declarant extends to every private business this rescission of signatures of suretyship including, but not limited to, every application for a bank account, individual and business, every application for any form of insurance, including life insurance, motor vehicles insurance, business insurance, and home insurance and every other application involved in any private business endeavor and/or private investment evidencing a signature of suretyship, every signature now being a signature of agency without recourse/without prejudice by the sole beneficiary, *nunc pro tunc ab initio*. There is no proof to the contrary;

This Declaration of Rescission of Surety is retroactive to the date of Date Filed w/registrar on COLB the date of the filing of the organic public record of Declarant's Certificate of Live Birth in the State of Oregon, County of Multnomah.

"Maxim: Equity regards as done that which ought to have been done."

Further Declarant Sayeth Naught.

I, First-Middle of the family Last, affirm under penalty of perjury, under the laws of the United States of America, that the foregoing is true and correct to the best of my knowledge and belief so help me God. [28 USC 1746(1)]

Executed this_____day of_____two thousand eighteen.

Without Prejudice

FULL ACCESS TO MALIK KILAM LEGACY COURSE STATUS CORRECTION CLASS

COPY AND PASTE THE LINK BELOW

https://drive.google.com/drive/folders/1s5sbglD9wp0bAIfQpy-M1qd5hJxF44Tg?usp=sharing

3. <u>**1099 OID Education**</u>

HJR 192 – TOOK AWAY GOLD IN EXCHANGE TO PREPAY ALL OF YOUR DEBTS PAST PRESENT AND FUTURE

IT IS NOT A TAX UNTIL YOU ASSESS THE TAX

WHY DO YOU HAVE TO ASSESS THE TAX?

BECAUSE YOU OWN THE CREDIT THE GOVERNMENT IS USING

 YOU ARE THE CREDITOR IN FACT.

YOU ARE IDENTIFIED AS THE PAYOR AND THEMSELVES AS THE RECEPIENT OF THE FUNDS (ON CORPORATE AND GOVERNMENT FILINGS)

PUBLICATION 1212

https://www.irs.gov/pub/irs-pdf/p1212.pdf

Publication 1212
(Rev. January 2010)
Cat. No. 61273T

Department
of the
Treasury
Internal
Revenue
Service

Guide to Original Issue Discount (OID) Instruments

Contents

Future Developments .....
What's New .....
Introduction .....
Definitions .....
Information on OID on the OID list .....
Information not on the OID list .....
Information for Brokers and Middlemen .....
Short-Term Obligations
Redeemed at Maturity .....
Long-Term Debt Instruments .....
Certificates of Deposit .....
Bearer Bonds and Coupons .....
Backup Withholding .....
Information for Owners of OID Debt Instruments .....
Form 1099-OID .....
How To Report OID .....
Figuring OID on Long-Term Debt Instruments .....
Figuring OID on Stripped Bonds and Coupons .....
How To Get Tax Help .....
Index .....

Future Developments

For the latest information about developments related to Pub. 1212, such as legislation enacted after it was published, go to www.irs.gov/pub1212.

What's New

Backup withholding. HM 115-97 lowered the backup from 28% to 24%. For more Backup Withholding, later.

Form 1099 filing requirement to report OID, you must file 1099, you must file 1040EZ for 2018, you can't use to report OID. See How To Report.

Photographs of Children

The IRS is a proud partner with the National Center for Missing & Exploited Children (NCMEC). Photographs of missing children selected by the Center may appear in this publication on pages that would otherwise be blank. You can help bring these children home by looking at the photographs and calling 1-800-THE-LOST (1-800-843-5678) if you recognize a child.

Get forms and other information faster and easier at:
IRS.gov (English)   IRS.gov/Korean (한국어)
IRS.gov/Spanish (Español)   IRS.gov/Russian (Pусский)
IRS.gov/Chinese (中文)   IRS.gov/Vietnamese (Tiếng Việt)

Jan 16, 2019

Nominee. If you are the holder of an OID debt instrument and you receive a Form 1099-OID that shows your taxpayer identification number and includes amounts belonging to another person, you are considered a "nominee." You must file another Form 1099-OID for each actual owner, showing the OID for the owner. Show the owner of the debt instrument as the "recipient" and you as the "payer." Complete Form 1099-OID and Form 1096 and file the forms with the Internal Revenue Service Center for your area. You must also give a copy of the

Form 1099-OID to the actual owner. However, you are not required to file a nominee return to show amounts belonging to your spouse. See the Form 1099 instructions for more information. When preparing your tax return, follow the

Nominee. If you are the holder of an OID debt instrument and you receive a Form 1099-OID that shows your taxpayer identification number and includes amounts belonging to another person, you are considered a "nominee." You must file another Form 1099-OID for each actual owner, showing the OID for the owner. Show the owner of the debt instrument as the "recipient" and you as the "payer."

Complete Form 1099-OID and Form 1096 and file the forms with the Internal Revenue Service Center for your area. You must also give a copy of the Form 1099-OID to the actual owner. However, you are not required to file a nominee return to show amounts belonging to your spouse. See the Form 1099 instructions for more information.

When preparing your tax return, follow the instructions under *Showing an OID adjustment* in the next discussion.

instructions under Showing an OID adjustment in the next discussion.

A. Who Must File

See the separate specific instructions for each form.

Nominee/middleman returns.

Generally, if you receive a Form 1099 for amounts that actually belong to another person, you are considered a nominee recipient. You must file a Form 1099 with the IRS (the same type of Form 1099 you received) for each of the other owners showing the amounts allocable to each. You also must furnish a Form 1099 to each of the other owners. File the new Form 1099 with Form 1096 with the Internal Revenue Service Center for your area. On each new Form 1099, list yourself as the "payer" and the other owner as the "recipient." On Form 1096, list yourself as the "Filer." A spouse is not required to file a nominee return to show amounts owned by the other spouse. The nominee, not the original payer, is responsible for filing the subsequent Forms 1099 to show the amount allocable to each owner.

Successor/predecessor reporting.

A successor business entity (a corporation, partnership, or sole proprietorship) and a predecessor business entity (a corporation, partnership, or sole proprietorship) may agree that the successor will assume all or some of the predecessor's information reporting responsibilities. This would permit the successor to file one Form 1097, 1098, 1099, 3921, 3922, 5498, or W-2G for each recipient combining the predecessor's and successor's reportable amounts, including any withholding. If they so agree and the successor satisfies the predecessor's obligations and the conditions described on this page, the predecessor does not have to file the specified information returns for the acquisition year. If the successor and predecessor do not agree, or if the requirements described are not met, the predecessor and the successor each must file Forms 1097, 1098, 1099, 3921, 3922, 5498, and W-2G for their own reportable amounts as they usually would. For more information and the rules that apply to filing combined Forms 1042-S, see Rev. Proc. 99-50, which is available on page 757 of Internal Revenue Bulletin 1999-52 at IRS.gov/pub/irs-irbs/irb99-52.pdf.

WHAT ARE THE AMOUNTS BELONGING TO ANOTHER PERSON?

THAT IS THE AMOUNT OF THE BILLS (DEBT INSTRUMENTS) FROM THE CORPORATIONS AND BANKS EVERY MONTH FOR THE USE OF YOUR CREDIT AS A NOMINEE FOR YOU.

YOU ARE THE PAYOR AND BENEFICIAL OWNER BECAUSE THEY ARE USING YOUR TRUST'S AND SOLE PROP'S CREDIT AND IT DOES NOT BECOME A TAX UNTIL YOU ASSESS IT. AND THE WAY YOU ASSESS IT IS BY FILING FORMS

PAY TO THE ORDER OF US DEPARTMENT OF TREASURY

Study Material ONLY, think and draw your own conclusion.
Everything in life is a voluntary process, take RESPONSIBILITY for it!!
Life is what we make it, Always has been, always will be. *–Grandma Moses*
A republican form of government is not a spectator sport.
Vengeance: the best manner of avenging ourselves is by not resembling him who has injured us. By Jane Porter

#1 = is TAXES

Taxes supercede Contract law, because of your Treasury direct account (your SS#) due to the Bankruptcy.

Always address every issue in (COURT) as a **TAX ISSUE!!!** You're not in law. **YOU'RE IN TAX COURT.**

THERE'S *NO MONEY* "ONLY TAXES".

A Bill is a Money Order, from them.

We never make anyone offers.
We let them make the offer.
They get the originals back! You make copies for yourself!!
YOU DON'T GO TO JAIL FOR FILING YOUR TAXES!!!

#2 = is CONTRACT LAW

1) Oral Contract, written contract and PERFORMANCE Contract.

2) Performance Contract is the most damaging to us. If we act like defendant and argue Law or resist zeroing our account, we are in Commercial Dishonor.

↓   ↓   ↓   ↓

"YOUR TOAST" AND MAY GO TO JAIL.

Forms to be ordered
1-800-829-3676
1099 O.I.D.
1096
        Order forms for years 2001 and current year Because if you run out of the forms you need (current year) the 1 can be changed into any number you need.

2

HJR-192, JUNE 5, 1933 =debt instrument   FEDERAL GOV'T   STATE GOV'T   CORPORATIONS
                                       Debtor   Debtor   Debtor

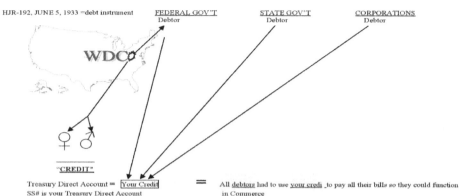

"CREDIT"

Treasury Direct Account = [Your Credit]   **=**   All debtors had to use your credit to pay all their bills so they could function
SS# is your Treasury Direct Account   in Commerce
And your Name.

Your Credit, when used by anyone (you or them)   HJR-192
Has to be reported as your (taxable) income on a   the product is already paid for because they used your credit to build
1040 and 1099 O.I.D.,1096 and 1040-V to the IRS every year and pay for it, however, the Bill is a new offer, and it tells us how much of
                                              our credit they used

Your Treasury Direct Account must be kept at ZERO,
just like your checkbook.
This is why you have to file your taxes

HJR-192 automatically extended the privilege to renege on debts to every person using the Federal Reserve banking system;
however, never forget that when you operate on a privilege, you have to respect the ruler of the giver of that privilege.
Furthermore, in the case of Great Falls Mfg. Co. v. Attorney General, 124 U.S. 581, the court said: "The court will not pass upon
the constitutionality of a statute at the instance of one who has availed himself of its benefits."

Thus, if you avail yourself of any benefits of the public credit system you waive the right to challenge the validity of any statute
pertaining to, and conferring "benefits" of this system on the basis of constitutionality

Sample: The States figured out the easiest way too use our Credit to pay their bills, build roads, schools, courthouses, etc.
They decided that the easiest way was to use Block(ed) Grants. A Block (Ed) Grant = they block us from using our
Credit, but they use it! All merchants use Blocked Grants against us when they don't send a check.

      When anyone uses our Credit, (you & them), we as owners (Principal) of our Treasury Direct Account (our SS#
and your Name) have to report this taxable income every year on a 1040, 1099 O.I.D. and 1096, 1040-V.

      The County Attorney in every State writes a check for the entire county's needs, and signs your name to it, by
assumption.
      By signing your name it looks like you have income in the amount of the check. All income has to be reported to
the IRS on a 1040, 1099 O.I.D., 1096 and 1040-V. All governments and Corporations use this method. The only way
we know who is definitely using our credit is when we get a bill in the mail or receipt from them.

      Once you file your yearly 1040, 1099 O.I.D., 1096 and 1040-V., the IRS will pull all of your credit from everyone
who has used it under your (Trust Account) Treasury Direct Account # (your SS #), even the ones you do not know
about. If you do not file every year, your Treasury Direct Account shows you didn't declare all your taxable income
(credit); therefore you are a tax delinquent fugitive, which is a **CRIMINAL** charge.
File your taxes to get your Credit back = REFUND

Why this is not Fraud
On their first offer to us, it may be an offer to enable us to obtain our Credit back on the 1040, 1099 O.I.D., 1096 and
1040-V forms. (Contract Law)
      Having assumed the use of our Credit is not Fraud. The only error by them is that they assume that our income

Who is the dept. of the Treasury, Internal Revenue Service?

They are the bookkeepers for your credit, your Treasury Direct Account (your SS#). Your Treasury Direct Account is just like your checkbook. It must be kept within a reasonable balance. The IRS will send you a bill if it gets to far on the taxable income side, out of balance. The 1040, 1099 O.I.D., 1096 and 1040-V is filed every year brings your Treasury direct Account back to ZERO.

It is your account and your responsibility to keep your account within reason. YOUR CREDIT IS TAXBLE INCOME = YOU HAVE TO DECLARE YOUR INCOME!! The use of your credit has to be reported, weather you use it or they use it.

If you don't keep your Treasury Direct Account at zero yearly, they may charge you with "criminal charges" and hold your body as collateral until you zero out your Treasury Direct Account, because you are a tax delinquent FUGITIVE!

ALL TAXES ARE FEDERAL TAXES; there is no such thing as a State tax.

The truth on your tax return can only be agreed to by another 1040 or 1040-V. If anyone tries to invent a false claim on a 1040 or 1040-V, it would be perjury. Otherwise all he/she could do is agree with you, and that makes it a civil matter. That's why any assumed agreement must go on a 1040 or 1040-V to compel someone to commit perjury.

Debts cannot be written off until they have been charged ASSESSED as a tax on the 1040 or 1040-V. The Corporations cannot charge or assess taxes. They can collect them, but they can't write off tax loses because they cannot assess them. They need the accused person to NOT ASSESS the tax, which is a commercial Protest/Dishonor/Default.

(Credit) that they use is tax exempt. It's not tax-exempt until we tax it by filing our 1040, 1099 O.I.D., 1096 and 1040-V

Things to watch for and to do: Once you're up-to-date with filing your yearly taxes

ATTENTION: KEEP THE ENVELOPES. THEY ARE YOUR FIRST OFFER FROM THEM. IE THE I.R.S.

1. This Red Postage Stamp is also a Bill/Money Order = $300.00 penalty for private use.
2. Red Postage Stamp or Black under who sent it = $600.00 (penalty for private use) + red postage fee. This is a new offer to offset your original offer. Once you have filed your 1040, 1099 O.I.D., 1096 and 1040-V with the IRS, and if they send you a new offer with the red postage statement on it, write on the envelope: "Pay to the United States Treasury" and attach a 1040-V for the $300.00 + the postage fee and if there is red and black penalty for private use it's $600.00 + the postage fee if any. Return the envelope and 1040-V and their copy of the 1099 O.I.D. back to whomever sent it to you
3. OPEN THE ENVELOPE. Check for duplicate offers in the envelope. (See # 6)
4. The only way they can get out of this is to try to contract with us by making us new offers to offset their original offer
5. Whoever answers last "wins" – we always answer their offers in 10 days. (Truth in lending)
6. Don't forget to write your account # (your SS#) on the envelope and your name. See page 9 for the money order
7. If there are 2 or 3 identical offers in one envelope it means that its 2 x $600.00 = $1200.00 plus postage fee. Put a real persons name on the money order on the envelope i.e. The head of the agency if there are no names in the envelope. Do the 1040-V for the amount of the postage.
8. They need the penalty for private use to do private business with us.

Things we NEVER do:
1. We don't sue for damages.
2. We don't make them offers.
3. We don't argue any issue, we just zero out the account for settlement and closing in exchange Treasury Direct # your SS#)

We don't file lawsuits, because you would be making them an offer.

When using the Pay to the United States Treasury on a Bill along with the 1040-V, this is the streamlined version. This means you have to assessed/charged the tax/account and it goes to zero. The 1040-V is a tax return which assesses/charges the account. It replaces the long 1040 form, and is used for a particular issue.

MONEY ORDER, when using the money order on a bill along with the 1040-V. Send the originals to IRS along with the original 1040-V. Send copy to whomever sent the bill. You have the option of doing the 1099 O.I.D. and 1096.

1099 O.I.D. Identifies me as the sponsor of the credit that funded the treasury "bill" in the first place, and is also taking the bill to exempt status. (Use for any $ claims)

1040 used for your yearly, quarterly tax return along with the 1099 O.I.D., 1096 and 1040-V

1040-V used for a particular issue (bill) through out the year, but you can use this for every bill you get. Study the transcript on this. Both the 1040 and the 1040-V are a tax return which charges/assess the bill/tax for a refund/ return to source. The Bill/account has to be "charged: on a 1040 or 1040-V for a return to source. These (2) documents assess the taxable income that is in any/all accounts. The 1040 assessment is the charge to zero the account. **ASSESSED AND CHARGED AS A TAX, BECAUSE THERE IS NO MONEY. Only debt/credit.**

The 1040-V, statement you send with your Check or money Order for any balance due on the "Amount owed". (For any Bill the SURETY (strawman). Make money order payable to the United States treasury.

1. The original offer.

   Do the 1040-V for the amount of the money offer, do the Money Order on their Bill and any envelope that has the fee Penalty for private use on it.

   EXAMPLE

          Money Order   Date:

   Pay (print out the dollar amount) $XXX.XX
   Pay to the United States Treasury and
   Charge the same to (to their name)
   Address you are sending it to.
   Memo Account: XXX-XX-XXX   Authorized Representative By: Your name

Note: Always sign your name on the right hand side of the money order this is the Creditor/principal side

CREDIT SIDE 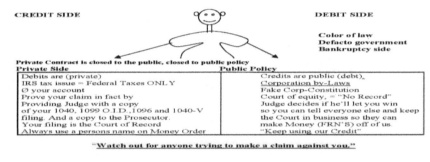 DEBIT SIDE

Color of law
Defacto government
Bankruptcy side

Private Contract is closed to the public, closed to public policy

Private Side	Public Policy
Debits are (private)	Credits are public (debt)_
IRS tax issue = Federal Taxes ONLY	Corporation by-Laws
Ø your account	Fake Corp-Constitution
Prove your claim in fact by	Court of equity, = "No Record"
Providing Judge with a copy	Judge decides if he'll let you win
of your 1040, 1099 O.I.D.,1096 and 1040-V	so you can tell everyone else and keep
filing. And a copy to the Prosecutor.	the Court in business so they can
Your filing is the Court of Record	make Money (FRN'S) off of us.
Always use a persons name on Money Order	"Keep using our Credit"

"Watch out for anyone trying to make a claim against you."

(You can do the 1099 O.I.D. it's up to you.) If your not in a Court Case, send the Original documents to the IRS and send a copy to the person who sent the bill, the treasury will pull your credit from whoever made the original offer. Don't worry about your copy when you are in court…it's your account so you can handle your private matters how you want to.

2. I would suggest that you take care of your Federal and State Tax bills by doing the yearly 1040 long form filing first to clean up your account, but these are private decisions that you must make yourself.

++
++

THE SIMPLE VERSION

EXAMPLE

          Money Order   Date:
Pay   (print out the dollar amount) $XXX.XX
Pay to the United States Treasury
Memo Account: XXX-XX-XXX   Authorized Representative By: Your name

And do the 1040- V

++
++

"IF WE DECIDE TO PAY THE BILL DURING THE YEAR"

Write the Money Order on their bill/envelope
Do a 1040-V for amount of the bill/envelope
Do a 1099 O.I.D. for amount of the bill/envelope
Do a 1096 for amount of the bill/envelope

1. They (whoever made the offer) gets back their original bill, original 1040-V and copy of the 1099 O.I.D.

2. Send IRS Kansas city, MO 64999 (if you live in Michigan)
The Red 1099 O.I.D.
The red 1096.
1040-V.
Their offer.

"KEEP and MAKE COPIES FOR YOURSELF"

9

Latest revision March 18, 2007. NOTICE: We are not attorneys nor are we acting in any capacity as legal counsel. The information provided within these pages is intended for the edification of the reader only (for entertainment purposes only) and while we believe this information to be true and correct it is not offered in any way as legal advice. Therefore, it is entirely up to the reader to seek appropriate legal advice before acting upon any information contained in these pages.

Use these two letters below, when you are sending your first filing to the IRS

Your address
Town , MI 484XX
Date:

Do Not Staple   6769

| Form **1096**
 Department of the Treasury
 Internal Revenue Service | **Annual Summary and Transmittal of**
 U.S. Information Returns | OMB No. 1545-0108
 2006 |

FILER'S name

YOUR NAME

Street address (including room or suite number)

STREET ADDRESS

City, state, and ZIP code
CITY STATE AND ZIP

| Name of person to contact
 YOUR NAME | Telephone number
 ( ) ------------------ | **For Official Use Only** |
| Email address
 ------------------------ | Fax number
 ( ) ------------------ | |

| 1 Employer identification number
 W/O DASHES XXXXXXXXX | 2 Social security number
 W/DASHES XXX-XX-XXXX | 3 Total number of forms TOTAL # OF PAGES | 4 Federal income tax withheld
 $ TOTAL ALL 1099 OID | 5 Total amount reported with this Form 1096
 $ FROM BOX 4 |

Enter an "X" in only one box below to indicate the type of form being filed.   If this is your **final return**, enter an "X" here . . . ▶ [X]

W-2G 32	1098 81	1098-C 78	1098-E 84	1098-T 83	1099-A 80	1099-B 79	1099-C 85	1099-CAP 73	1099-DIV 91	1099-G 86	1099-H 71	1099-INT 92	1099-LTC 93
☐	☐	☐	☐	☐	☐	☐	☐	☐	☐	☐	☐	☐	☐

1099-MISC 95	1099-OID 96	1099-PATR 97	1099-Q 31	1099-R 98	1099-S 75	1099-SA 94	5498 28	5498-ESA 72	5498-SA 27
☐	[X]	☐	☐	☐	☐	☐	☐	☐	☐

Return this entire page to the Internal Revenue Service. Photocopies are not acceptable.

Under penalties of perjury, I declare that I have examined this return and accompanying documents, and, to the best of my knowledge and belief, they are true, correct, and complete.

Signature ▶ By: YOUR NAME   Title ▶ AUTHORIZED REPRESENTATIVE   Date ▶ DATE

Instructions

Purpose of form. Use this form to transmit paper Forms 1099, 1098, 5498, and W-2G to the Internal Revenue Service. Do not use Form 1096 to transmit electronically or magnetically. For magnetic media, see Form 4804, Transmittal of Information Returns Reported Magnetically; for electronic submissions, see Pub. 1220, Specifications for Filing Forms 1098, 1099, 5498, and W-2G Electronically or Magnetically.

Who must file. The name, address, and TIN of the filer on this form must be the same as those you enter in the upper left area of Forms 1099, 1098, 5498, or W-2G. A filer includes a payer; a recipient of mortgage interest payments (including points) or student loan interest; an educational institution; a broker; a barter exchange; a creditor; a person reporting real estate transactions; a trustee or issuer of any individual retirement arrangement, a Coverdell ESA, an HSA, an Archer MSA (including a Medicare Advantage MSA); certain corporations; certain donees of motor vehicles, boats, and airplanes; and a lender who acquires an interest in secured property or who has

When to file. File Form 1096 as follows.
- With Forms 1099, 1098, or W-2G, file by February 28, 2007.
- With Forms 5498, 5498-ESA, or 5498-SA, file by May 31, 2007.

Where To File

Except for Form 1098-C, send all information returns filed on paper with Form 1096 to the following:

If your principal business, office or agency, or legal residence in the case of an individual, is located in	Use the following Internal Revenue Service Center address
Alabama, Arizona, Arkansas, Connecticut, Delaware, Florida, Georgia, Kentucky, Louisiana, Maine, Massachusetts, Mississippi, New Hampshire, New Jersey, New Mexico, New York, North Carolina, Ohio, Pennsylvania, Rhode Island, Texas,	Austin, TX 73301

Having them file for you

If you are not sure about the above way to file, then put all your receipts, 1099, W-2, whatever you want to file with them into an envelope of proper size, make sure that you keep a copy for yourself and send this letter with the receipts,1099, W-2, whatever you want to file with them which instructs the IRS to file for you. Simple and safe!!

Dear Whomever,   Date: xxxxx

     As the Principal and owner of Treasury Direct Account #XXX-XX-XXXX, Your name   I request you file the Federal tax forms 1040/1099 O.I.D. and 1096 for tax period(s)Year(s) in question and any other returns that are due for me.

     Please file the liabilities as taxable income to me, but omit filing or posting deductions against the taxable income to me or making adjustments to dilute the liability on taxable income as, that is a conflict of interest. This request is for return for settlement and closing in exchange Treasury Direct Account # XXX-XX-XXXX.

     On the 1099 O.I.D. the correction box at the top should be checked and also the Treasury Direct Number #XXX-XX-XXXX is to be placed as the account number at the bottom of the 1099 O.I.D. form under Recipient to prevent identity theft and the account being intercepted and diverted (deferred) if left open.

                      By:_____
                      Authorized Representative

SIGNATURE GUARANTEED
MEDALLION GUARANTEED
LEGAL FIRM NAME

Authorized signature

(1234)

AUTHORIZED SIGNATI

X 1 2 3 4 5 6

SECURITIES TRANSFER AGENTS MEDALLION PROGI

MEDALLION STAMP OR BANKER SIGNATURE
GUARANTEED CAN BE OBTAINED FROM YOUR BANK FOR
FREE IN MOST CASES AND THIS ACTS AS A NOTARY BUT
FOR BANKING PURPOSES.

It's not the same as getting something notarized, the documents warned. A notary stamp verifies your identity when you sign legal documents, whereas a Medallion Signature Guarantee verifies your identity for the transfer of securities, like the tradable assets in your retirement account, for example. When you're preparing to move these funds, the bank officer who provides the stamp and signature is verifying your identity to the point where they'll guarantee the amount that's being transferred.

SECONDLY WHEN DEALING WITH CORPORATIONS YOU WANT TO MAKE AN INDVIDUAL LIABLE SO YOU
ALWAYS SEND YOUR DOCUMENTS VIA CERTIFIED POST THAT WAY YOU ALWAYS HAVE THE RIGHT TO
FACE YOUR ACCUSER AND YOU KNOW WHO IT IS.

THE US DEPARTMENT OF TREASURY IS THE
BOOKKEEPERS FOR THE UNITED STATES CORPORATION

UNLESS YOU RECORD THE RETURN OR THE TAX THEN
THEY CAN NOT DO THE BOOKKEEPING ON IT.

THAT'S WHY THE TREASURYS BOOKS ARE OFF BALANCED
THE PAYABLES AND RECEIVEABLES ARE OFF BALANCED
UP BECAUSE THEY CAN NOT PAY THE PAYABLES WHICH
IS DUE TO THE PEOPLE.

THEY CAN NOT PAY THE PEOPLE BECAUSE THEY HAVE NOT FILED THE CORRECT PAPERWORK TO GET THE REFUND ON THE CREDIT THAT THEY ARE GIVING AWAY

AFTER 36 MONTHS THE CORPORATIONS AND BANKERS COME IN AS THE NOMINEE AND USE YOUR TAX PAYER IDENTIFCATION NUMBER ON A 1099A UTLIZING THE DEBT INSTRUMENT AS ABANDONED PROPERTY BECAUSE YOU NEVER CLAIMED IT. WHO EVER CLAIMS IT OWNS IT

WE ALSO SEND THEM A BLANK W9 REQUESTING TO SEE THEIR TAX IDENTIFICATION NUMBER AS YOU FILL THIS OUT WHEN STARTING ANY NEW BANK ACCOUNT. WE ATTACH THIS TO ANY FORMS WHEN DEALING WITH CORPORATIONS UTLIZING OUR CREDIT.

THE AMOUNTS BELONGING TO ANOTHER PERSON IS THE AMOUNT OF THE CREDIT THEY ARE USING AND THAT SHALL BE REPRESENTED AS A TAX WHEN THE TAX IS ASSESSED IT THEN BECOMES A TAX ISSUE AND TAX MATTER AND THEN IT BECOMES A RETURN. WHEN YOU SHOW THE CORPORATIONS AS RECEIPENTS OF THE

FUNDS THEN THE IRS SHALL ISSUE YOU A REFUND. IF YOU DO NOT DO THIS THEN YOU ABANDON THE FUNDS AND THE 1099 A IS FILED BY THE CORPORATIONS AND THE FUNDS GOTO THE CORPORATION THAT FILED THE 1099 A. THE CORPORATIONS ARE ALWAYS FILING AS A NOMINEE FOR THE TRUE OWNER WHEN YOU SIGN OVER THE RIGHTS TO YOUR BUSINESS (YOUR NAME AND CREDIT).

EVERYTHING IS A TAX ISSUE UNDER THE BANKRUPTCY OF THE UNITED STATES CORPORATIONS.

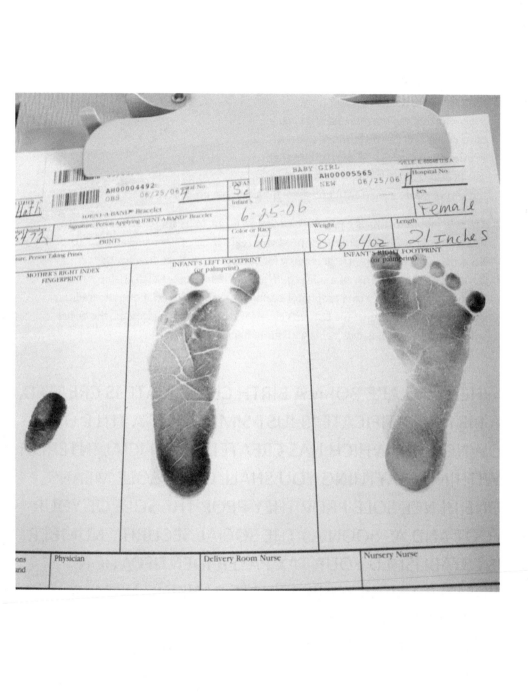

The sole proprietorship is the simplest business form under which one can operate a business. The sole proprietorship is not a legal entity. It simply refers to a person who owns the business and is personally responsible for its debts. A sole proprietorship can operate under the name of its owner or it can do business under a fictitious name, such as Nancy's Nail Salon. The fictitious name is simply a trade name-- it does not create a legal entity separate from the sole proprietor owner.

The sole proprietorship is a popular business form due to its simplicity, ease of setup, and nominal cost. A sole proprietor need only register his or her name and secure local licenses, and the sole proprietor is ready for business. A distinct disadvantage, however, is that the owner of a sole proprietorship remains personally liable for all the business's debts. So, if a sole proprietor business runs into financial trouble, creditors can bring lawsuits against the business owner. If such suits are successful, the owner will have to pay the business debts with his or her own money.

WHEN YOU ARE BORN A BIRTH CERTIFICATE IS CREATED. A BIRTH CERTIFICATE IS JUST SIMPLY PUT A TITLE OF OWNERSHIP WHICH HAS CREATED BENEFICIAL INTEREST WITHIN EVERYTHING YOU SHALL OWN. SOLE MEANS ONE HENCE SOLE PROP THEY PROP THE SOLE OF YOUR FOOT AND AS SOON AS THE SOCIAL SECURITY NUMBER IS ESTABLISHED YOUR TAX PAYER IDENTIFCATION NUMBER THIS IS YOUR PRIVATE BANKING NUMBER SET UP FOR THE SOCIALIST SECURITY ADMINISTRATION WHICH IS ANOTHER TRUST. THE BENEFITS ARE TIED TO YOU BEING ABLE TO UTILZE TRUST CERTIFICATE UNITS

FROM THE FEDERAL RESERVES WHICH IS UNDER THE IN GOD WE TRUST YES THAT IS THE NAME OF THEIR TRUST THE IN GOD WE.

THE CONSTITUTION IS CONSIDERED TO BE AN EXPRESSED TRUST. WHEN YOU GO INTO ANY COURT ROOM YOU ARE CREATING A CONSTRUCTIVE TRUST. THIS IS A DIFFERENT TOPIC FOR A DIFFERENT BOOK BUT AS OF RIGHT NOW LETS STICK TO THE SOLE PROP BUSINESS AND THE TAX.

28 U.S. Code § 3002. Definitions

(2) "Court" means any court created by the Congress of the United States, excluding the United States Tax Court.

(3) "Debt" means—

(A) an amount that is owing to the United States on account of a direct loan, or loan insured or guaranteed, by the United States; or

AS YOU CAN SEE ALL COURTS ARE TAX COURTS AND ALL DEBTS
ARE OWED TO THE UNITED STATES CORPORATION. IF YOU
CONTINUE TO READ TO SECTION 15 YOU SHALL SEE THAT THE
UNITED STATES IS INDEED A CORPORATION.

(4) "Debtor" means a person who is liable for a debt or against w
claim for a debt.

(5) "Disposable earnings" means that part of earnings remaining
deductions required by law have been withheld.

(6) "Earnings" means compensation paid or payable for personal
denominated as wages, salary, commission, bonus, or otherwise,
periodic payments pursuant to a pension or retirement program.

(7) "Garnishee" means a person (other than the debtor) who has
thought to have, possession, custody, or control of any property ir
debtor has a substantial nonexempt interest, including any obligat
debtor or to become due the debtor, and against whom a garnishr
section 3104 or 3205 is issued by a court.

(9) "Nonexempt disposable earnings" means 25 percent of disposable earnings, subject to section 303 of the Consumer Credit Protection Act.

(10) "Person" includes a natural person (including an individual Indian), a corporation, a partnership, an unincorporated association, a trust, or an estate, or any other public or private entity, including a State or local government or an Indian tribe.

(11) "Prejudgment remedy" means the remedy of attachment, receivership, garnishment, or sequestration authorized by this chapter to be granted before judgment on the merits of a claim for a debt.

(12) "Property" includes any present or future interest, whether legal or equitable, in real, personal (including choses in action), or mixed property, tangible or intangible, vested or contingent, wherever located and however held (including community property and property held in trust (including spendthrift and pension trusts)), but excludes—

(13) "Security agreement" means an agreement that creates or provides for a lien.

(14) "State" means any of the several States, the District of Columbia, the Commonwealth of Puerto Rico, the Commonwealth of the Northern Marianas, or any territory or possession of the United States.

(15) "United States" means—

(A) a Federal corporation;

(B) an agency, department, commission, board, or other entity of the United States; or

(C) an instrumentality of the United States.

(16) "United States marshal" means a United States marshal, a deputy marshal, or an official of the United States Marshals Service designated under section 564.

ALSO A NOTE TO MENTION SECTION 10 PERSON MEANS CORPORATION. THEN AGAIN THIS WHY YOU ARE CONSIDERED

A SOLE PROP CORPORATION AND YOUR BODY, LABOR AND EVEN WELL BEING CAN BE ATTACHED AS COLLATERAL FOR ANY MISHAPS OF THE BUSINESS DUE TO YOU NOT HAVING PROPER STANDING BY UPDATING YOUR STATUS WHICH WE HIGHLY RECOMMEND YOU DO BEFORE MOVING FORWARD WITH ANY 1099 OID PROCESS. WE ALSO HAVE ANOTHER BOOK ON HOW TO UPDATE YOUR STATUS PROPERLY ON THE PUBLIC SIDE AND THE PRIVATE SIDE.

AS YOUR BIRTH CERTIFICATE IS THE TITLE THAT SHOWS BENEFICIAL OWNERSHIP SO THIS IS THE PRIVATE SIDE. THE PUBLIC SIDE IS THE MONEY HOW ARE YOU ACTING IN WHAT CHARACTER OR TITLE ARE YOU ACTING FROM. WITH A SOCIAL YOU ARE A SLAVE. AS SOCIAL WORK FOR THE EIN THE EMPLOYER IDENTIFICATION NUMBER. EMPLOYEES ARE SLAVES AND THE EMPLOYERS ARE THE MASTERS. AS THE SOCIAL NUMBER AS WORKS FOR THE EIN.

FROM A LIMITED LIABILTY COMPANY YOU WOULD ACT FROM A MEMBER OR JUST AN AUTHORIZED REPRESENTIVE SO TO SPEAK. WITH CORPORATIONS YOU ACT FORM A CHIEF EXECUTIVE STANDPOINT OR EVEN PRESIDENT OR VICE PRESIDENT. FROM THE TRUST STANDPOINT YOU ALWAYS OPERATE FROM THE GRANTOR OR ADMINSTRATOR WHEN DEALING WITH YOUR PRIVATE AFFAIRS WITHIN A PUBLIC PLAY.

CLICK THE LINK BELOW TO GET ACCESS TO THE FULL 1099 OID MALIK KILAM LEGACY COURSE

https://drive.google.com/drive/folders/1jEOEQpy90gNP 5M3qsZlrKfte08jHselN?usp=sharing

CLICK THE LINK BELOW TO GET ACCESS TO THE FULL 1099 OID EBOOK
https://drive.google.com/file/d/15rcNbsdDmSBAslvhDcq k0KgC-xRwYmPH/view?usp=sharing

CLICK THE LINK BELOW TO GET ACCESS TO THE FULL ACCESS TO YOUR UNLIMITED CREDITS TREASURY DIRECT LEGACY ACCOUNT ESTABLISHMENT

https://drive.google.com/file/d/1ftnbu5Fdx_oYIDcKap0- J3a8VFTLfWsa/view?usp=sharing

4.   <u>Personal Debt Elimination</u>

Let's have a little quiz: 1. Who meets at the House Of Parliament in London England?

2. What do they do there?

3. Do they help you in any way? If your answers were:

1. "Members of the government"

2. "They represent all the people living in the country" and

3. "Yes, they create laws to protect me and my family. Then let me congratulate you on getting every one of the answers wrong. Didn't do too well on that quiz? OK, let's have another go:

4. When was slavery abolished?

5. Was slavery legal?

6. Are you in debt to a financial institution? Here are the answers:

1. The serving officers of a commercial company.

2. They think up ways to take money and goods from you.

3. No, absolutely not, they help themselves and not you.

4. Slavery has NEVER been abolished and you yourself, are considered to be a slave right now.

5. Yes, slavery is "legal" although it is not "lawful" (you need to discover the difference).

6. No. You are NOT in debt to any financial institution.

Does this seem a little strange to you? If it does, then read on: THOSE IN POWER HAVE A BIG SECRET Paying tax is OPTIONAL !! Registering a vehicle is OPTIONAL !! Paying a fine is OPTIONAL !! Attending a court is OPTIONAL !! YOU CAN IF YOU WANT TO, BUT YOU DON'T HAVE TO Surprised? Well – try this for size: Every Mortgage and Loan is FULLY REPAID from day one – you can pay it again if you want to, but you don't have to !!

READ MEET YOUR STRAWMAN PDF BY CLICKING THE LINK BELOW

https://fouryoureyesonlyoo7.files.wordpress.com/2011/06/strawman.pdf

DON KILAM'S HAND CRAFTED DISPUTE AFFIDAVIT FOR REGULAR LOANS AND DEBTS

NON-NEGOTIABLE

_____in the tribe _____
c/o _____

_____
_____
Republic States United

CC: ATTENTION: _____
c/o_____,
_____
_____

Re: Account Number: _____

Mister or Misses _____
I would be happy to settle any financial obligation I might lawfully owe, as soon as I have received the following documentation from you:

1. Validation of the debt (the actual accounting);
2. Verification of your claim against me (a sworn affidavit or a hand signed invoice in accordance with The Bills of Exchange Act (1882)); Uniform Commerical Codes, Federal Fair Credit Reporting Act, and Georgia State Statues for Lawful Purposes.
3.A copy of the contract signed by both parties and therefore binding both parties.
4.Please also provide me with a true and certified copy (NOT photocopy) of the Original Note (Credit Agreement), under penalty of perjury and with unlimited liability and confirm that this Note, has never been sold.
5. Please also confirm the name of the individual who is the duly authorized representative from your company, who has carried out due diligence under The Money Laundering Regulations 2007 and what actions s/he has taken in relation to this account.

I hereby give you ten (10) days to reply to this notice from the above date with a notice sent using recorded post and signed under full commercial liability and penalties of perjury, assuring and promising me that all of the replies and details given to the above requests are true and without deception, fraud or mischief. Your said failure to provide the aforementioned documentation within ten (10) days, from the above date, to validate the debt, will constitute your agreement to the following terms:

That the debt did not exist in the first place;
OR

It has already been paid in full;
AND
That any damages suffer, you will be held culpable;
That any negative remarks made to a credit reference agency will be removed;
You will no longer pursue this matter any further.
You agree to pay all fee schedules.

Please Note: I wish to deal with this matter in writing and I do not give your organization permission to contact me by telephone. Should you do so, I must warn you that the calls could constitute 'harassment' and I may take action under Section 1 of the Protection from Harassment Act 1997 and the Administration of Justice Act 1970 S.40, which makes it a Criminal Offence for a creditor or a creditor's agent to make demands (for money), which are aimed at causing 'alarm, distress or humiliation', because of their frequency or manner.

STATMENT OF FACTS

For the record we wish to effect payment immediately. What is the sum certain on the penal funds?

Affiant is a national of the nation/state_____, as contemplated by the act of congress evidenced and restated at 8 U.S.C. 1101(a)(2). Affiant is aware and knows that the U.S. bankruptcy is verified in Senate Report No. 93-519 93rd. Congress, 1st Session (1973), Summary of Emergency Power Statues, "Executive Orders 6073, 6102, 6111, and by Executive Order 6260 on March 9th, 1933 under the "Trading with the Enemy Act (Sixty-Fifth Congress, Session 1, Chapters 105, 106, October 6th, 1917, and as further codified at 12 U.S.C.A. 95(a) and (b) as amended.

- I conditionally accept all facts in the claim if the respondent can prove authority to make presentments
- I conditionally accept for value and return for value the presumption I have a duty to show cause for actions upon proof of claim that it is not public policy of the **UNITED STATES** under **HJR-192** *to not pay debts at law but instead to exchange consideration upon a dollar for dollar basis to discharge or offset a liability.*
- I conditionally accept for value and return for value the presumption I have a duty to show cause for my actions with the bank or respondent upon proof of claim that without money of account (*as established under **Article One, Sections 10**, clause one, of the Organic Constitution of the Untied States of America*) in circulation that the only commercial consideration that exists is each and every person's exemption by way of a prepaid account operated by the United States Secretary of Treasury.

Affiant is aware and knows that a certificate of live birth (certificate of title) is a bond that evidences title held by the **Depositary Trust Company (DTCC).** The issuer has legal title; you have equitable title up until you partner up to share equitable title with the United States. SS-5 creates the UPPERCASE NAME which is surety for the Vessel. The Vessel is the body and evidenced on the application by length, weight, and footprints. A body manifested into the sea of commerce. The beneficiary is supposed to be Me, Myself, and I. But the Depositary Trust Company (DTCC) is at 55 Water Street New York City and operates both the public and the private side. Under Civil Rico Racketeering Laws **18 U.S.C.** 1964 as corporations may have established a pattern of racketeering activity by using mail to collect an unlawful debt. If proven there is a conspiracy to deprive of property without due process is various constitutional injuries under **18 U.S.C.A. 241**. *Knowledge and neglect to prevent a United States Constitutional* *wrong. 31 U.S.C. 5118 (d)2 None can ask for payment in specific coin. 31 U.S.C. 3123* There is no money, so no one can demand payment... the United States will discharge debt dollar for dollar.

Affiant is aware and knows that legal tender (FEDERAL RESERVE NOTES) are not good and lawful money of the United States. See **Rains V. State,State, 226 S.W .18**

Affiant is aware and knows that the Undersigned affiant has been estopped from using and has no access to ' lawful Constitutional Money of exchange' (see U.S. Constitution- Article 1 Section 10) to "pay debts at law", and pursuant to HJR-192, can only discharge fines, fees, debts, and judgements 'dollar for dollar' via commercial paper or upon Affiant's Exemption.

There are no judicial courts in America and there has no been since 1789. Judges do no enforce statutes and codes. Executive Administrators enforce statutes and codes. (**FRC V. GE 281 US464 KELLER V. PE 261 US 428, 1 STAT. 138-178**

I HEREBY notice that I am the executor of the Cestui Que Vie Trust of

_____

according to Title 26 sections 303 & 7701, companies, corporations, and associations and trusts are all decedents. This means my all UPPERCASE NAME IS A LEGAL ESTATE. My ALL UPPERCASE NAME falls into this class. I direct all of the affairs and financial affairs of _____

The following documents are needed to move forward in these matters
All tax bond receipts 1099 OID, 1099A, 1099C

The authorization from the INTERNAL REVENUE SERVICE to go forward with the above mentioned account number [26 U.S.C. 2032A(e)11]
Employee Affidavit [Title 5 U.S.C. 3333]
Registration [Title 22 U.S.C. 611 and 612]

Please provide all of the following information and submit the appropriate forms and paperwork back to me along with an affidavit signed in accordance with 28 U.S.C. 1746 for validation and proof of claim.

I affirm that all statement, facts, and information presented in this affidavit/ writ are correct and are presented as evidence for the record. Evidence, exhibit, Information, and facts are placed in Evidence in this case, and As I am reserving and retaining all my rights and affirm to the best of my knowledge and belief.

MAY ALL PARTIES BE MINDFUL OF 48 CFR, 48 U.S.C., UNIFORM COMMERICAL CODES 1-308, 3-402, 3-419 3-501,

Affiant is aware and know that the various and numerous references to case law, legislative history, state and federal statutes/ codes, Federal Reserve Bank Publications, Supreme Court decisions, the Uniform Commercial Codes, U.S. Organic Constitutional, and general recognized maxims of Law as cited herein and throughout establish the following:

A) That the U.S. Federal government and the several United States did totally and completely debase the organic Lawful Constitutional Coin of the several States of the Union of the United States.

B) That the Federal Government and the several United States have and continue to breach the express mandates of Article 1 Section 10 of the Federal Constitution regarding the minting and circulation of lawful coin.
C) That the lawful coin (i.e. organic medium of exchange) and the former ability to PAY DEBTS has been replaced with fiat, paper currency, with the limited capacity to only discharge debts.
D) That Congress of the United States did legislate and provide the American People a remedy/ means to discharge all debt "dollar for dollar" via HJR-192 due to the declared Bankruptcy of the Corporate United States via the abolishment of Constitutional Coin and Currency.
No Assured value, no liability, errors, nor omissions excepted. All rights reserved and retain without recourse-non-assumpsit

FURTHER AFFIANT SAITH NOT.

Subscribed and sworn, without prejudice, and with all rights reserved,
(Printed Name:) _____

Principal, by Special Appearance, proceeding Sui Juris.
c/o _____
Republice in_____on or near [_____]

Signed:_____
Date:_____

On this_____day of_____,_____, before me, the undersigned, a Notary Public in and for _____, personally appeared the above-signed, known to me to be the one whose name is signed on this instrument, and has acknowledged to me that s/he has executed the same.

Signed:_____
Printed Name:_____
Date:_____
Address:_____

DON KILAM'S CAR OFFSET AFFIDAVIT

Certified Mail Receipt# _____
Return Receipt# _____

John Doe Smith
c/o 1000 Memorial Way apt 01
Moreno Valley, California Republic [0000]
Non-Resident/Non-Assumptic

October 9th, 2020

Mr. George Hurley, CEO/General Manager

c/o Mullen Financial
13672 Goldenwest St #H,
Westminster, CA 92683

Dear Mr. Hurley,

Would your accountant please prepare and file Federal Tax Form 1099 OID (Original Issue Discount) to cover the eligible issues (products of statues) for this
_____Account#:_____. The eligible issue in this matter consist of:

1. Department of Motor Vehicle Title for:
   Vehicle Description: _____
   VIN#:   _____

Please provide me with my copy of this **1099 OID form** as well as the forensic accounting, corresponding to **FinCEN Form 101, "Suspicious Activity Report"**.

The tax in question is the original issue discount. The filing of the 1099 OID is not mandatory on my part (voluntary), but, on request by me, becomes mandatory upon you and if not complied with, constitutes a "willful failure to file for income tax".

The filing of the 1099 OID is to enable the tax charge to return to the source for settlement and closing of escrow in exchange, Treasury Direct, SS# _____. After filing, please return to my possession all the corresponding property that belongs to me.

If a response is not received from you within (10) days of receipt of this letter, it will be assumed that you have chosen to dishonor me.

Sincerely,

JOHN DOE SMITH
AUTHRORIZED REP

Cc:

FORECLOSURE DISPUTE LETTER

Letter 1A - Affidavit Claim and Demand as the Creditor

NOTICE OF CLAIM AND GRIEVANCE/RESOLUTION REQUEST
NOTICE TO PRINCIPAL IS NOTICE TO
AGENT NOTICE TO AGENT IS NOTICE TO
PRINCIPAL

Timothy J. Mayopoulos, CEO, FNMA
3900 Wisconsin Ave NW Washington, DC 20016

Name, CEO, Mortgage Company Name
Company Address
NMLS ID # [I found this on the mortgage website]

RE: Alleged Account Number: [Mortgage Account #]; Property Address: [Your home address]; Tax ID: [Property Tax ID]; MIN: [Search for MERS # on https://www.mers-servicerid.org/sis/index]; Your County Circuit Court Case No.: [Foreclosure Case No]

I have discovered your habitual and extensive abuses with home loans and mortgage transactions associated with the above regarding. With the information I absorbed, the following has come to my attention:

1. The loan was personal.
2. The Note was never transferred to REMIC, thus it was was not secured.
3. I was an investor and I want my proceeds.
4. Home was paid for with the Mortgage Default Insurance.
5. I never abandoned my property, however, I rescind my consumer application due to unconscionable transaction, per 12 CFR Part 1026 (Regulation Z) 15(a)(2). Now you're in FTC and SEC Fraud.
6. By reporting anything but "debt is paid in full" you are open to lawsuit under the FDCPA.
7. I am the depositor and true creditor for this account, therefore you never risked any of your assets at any time AND you failed to provide disclosure.

Instead of reporting your Tax Fraud and over 19 counts of Title 18 crimes to the proper authorities exposing everyone involved to pay punitive, general, exemplary and special damages regarding the unlawful foreclosure, it would be beneficial if you return the property, my investment and damages you owe.

Self-Executing Contract
Co-Respondents voluntarily agree to report the account in the above Regarding to all credit bureaus as "paid as agreed" AND Repudiate Case No. [Foreclosure Court Case #] AND Reconvey the property to Claimant AND Compensate Claimant damages in the amount of $40,000,000.00 or .999 troy ounce in silver by certified mail within thirty (30) days from the date on this notice.

Equality under Law is PARAMOUNT and MANDATORY by Law. Silence equates to tacit agreement. It is my wish to resolve the matter without reporting or taking legal actions. However, your failure to respond in writing and comply within thirty (30) days I shall pursue all illegalities pursuant to the TRUTH-IN-LENDING ACT (TILA) §1602, §1635; U.C.C. ARTICLE 8 - INVESTMENT SECURITIES (1994) PART 5. SECURITY ENTITLEMENTS § 8-502., § 8-503., § 8-504., § 8-505., § 8-506., § 8-507., § 8-508., § 8-509 concurrently with Maryland Office of the Commissioner of Financial Regulation, IRS, SEC, OCC, Federal Reserve Board, FDIC and FDCPA § 1692 (e) (e(1-16)) (f) (f(1)) (f(6)) (g) (g(a)(1, 2, 3, 4)) (g(b)) ERROR RESOLUTION REQUEST UNDER 12 C.F.R. §1024.35, 12 CFR 226.39, Maryland Statutes Article § 3-105, 18 USC 1341, 18 USC 4, 15 USC 1692, 18 USC 287, 18 USC 1505, 18 USC 1623, 18 USC 1512, 18 USC 1021, 1028,1028a, 1038, over 19 counts of Title 18 crimes herein, including but not limited to: counterfeiting, conspiracy to defraud, illegal extortion of funds, breach of duty, commission and omission, defamation of character, false representation, fraud on the court, involuntary bankruptcy, mail fraud, purported credit limit, etc. This is a private communication and is intended to affect an out-of-court settlement of this matter. Conduct yourself accordingly.

I, :First-Middle: Last, Claimant, Affiant with all rights reserved, having personal knowledge and competent to testify to the above facts and declare the foregoing is true, correct and under the penalty of perjury.

Notary

by: _
:First-Middle: Last, *Sui*

*juris*_____
Your address

T: Your Telephone #

Letter 1B - Addendum of Agencies

ADDENDUM OF AGENCIES

TO:

Timothy J. Mayopoulos, CEO, FNMA
3900 Wisconsin Ave NW Washington, DC 20016

Via Registered U.S. Mail #:
Name, CEO, Mortgage Company Name
Company Address
NMLS ID # [I found this on the mortgage website]

Via Certified U.S. Mail #: _

RE: Alleged Account Number: [Mortgage Account #]; Property Address: [Your home address]; Tax ID: [Property Tax ID]; MIN: [Search for MERS # on https://www.mers-servicerid.org/sis/index]; Your County Circuit Court Case No.: [Foreclosure Case No]

U.S. Department of Treasury & FDIC

Notice of Insurance Violation pursuant to 12 U.S.C. § 1709 Section (9)(C)(ii) - Insurance of mortgages AND 12 U.S.C. § 3017 Section C - Bonds, debentures, notes and other evidences of indebtedness

U.S. Securities and Exchange Commission
REMIC Fraud Report

I.R.S. / CID Washington DC
IRS Form(s) 1041, 1066, 1099-A, <u>AND</u> 1099-OID

Maryland Secretary of State, Notary Division for Investigation
Investigation of Warranty Deed, Deed of Trust, Appointment of Substitute Trustee

U.S. District Court
Application for arrest warrants for offenses against the United States and equitable relief

Maryland Attorney General
Investigation of Breach of Oath, Power of Attorney, Securitization, Voidable Deed, Title 18 and Title 42
action violations

The agencies on this ADDENDUM will receive notice if/when you do not respond within 30 days of the
date on the NOTICE OF CLAIM AND GRIEVANCE/RESOLUTION REQUEST.

by:
:First-Middle: Last, *Sui juris*

Your address

T: Your Telephone #

CLICK THE LINK BELOW FOR ACCESS TO MALIK KILAM LEGACY COURSE MORTGAGE AND FORECLOSURE REDEMPTION

https://drive.google.com/drive/folders/1tGRBkYxrM9548R720CcpxaZtRvW4oZeQ?usp=sharing

Court Elimination

DIRECTIONS FOR CASES

GET DOCUMENTS NOTARAZIED

AFTER NOTARIZED

PUT TWO CENT STAMPS ON TOP OF DOCUMENTS

SIGN THRU THE STAMPS

SIGN THE BACK OF THE DOCUMENT LIKE A CHECK

SIGN AND DATE ALL RIGHTS RESERVED WITHOUT PREJUDICE

Attach form 56 fill out like illustration

Attach w9 and 1099 oid and the sf 28 forms are all left blank

Attach promissory note as well and sign and date back like a check

You no longer have to goto court return all mail to sender after blacking out YOUR NAME AS IT IS YOUR NAME AND CAN NOT BE USED WITHOUT YOUR PERMISSION

SEND CERTIFIED MAIL TO THE CLERK OF CLERKS

MAKE SURE TO SENT TO HER NAME

EXAMPLE

Jane Doe d/b/a Illinois County Clerk

This is not legal advice if you need legal advice please seek counsel this is for educational and informational and entertainment purposes only

CLICK LINK BELOW TO GET ACCESS TO COURT FILES AND TEMPLATES
https://drive.google.com/drive/folders/1eBiwvkd1Syq_rPdViVgJdXdiMfkjFPt_?usp=sharing

CLICK LINK BELOW FOR COLOR OF LAW AND COURT EDUCATION WITH MALIK KILAM LEGACY COURSE

https://drive.google.com/drive/folders/1iA8vpfgPv22pSoeAVdlCP0-wnvKKpn0r?usp=sharing

5. Bonds, Stocks, Notes & Securities

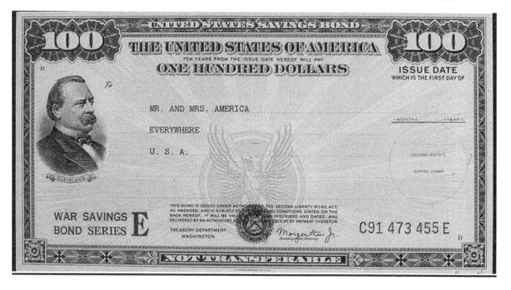

Bond for discharge

This is the creditor / holder's side of the bond (evidence of a debt). When you use a bond for discharge, you are

using your credit backed by the implied bond (debt) resulting from your pledges to help the US through its

bankruptcy. There is no value limit to this bond, as you voluntarily agree to pledge every bit of substance you

ever get until the money is put back into circulation. All the substance you have (cars, dirt, shoes, food,

toothbrushes) was acquired by giving the merchants Federal Reserve notes.

You can never get title to things unless you pay for them. Since there is no money in the US, only debt paper,

every time you get a pair of shoes, you are exchanging a debt for the shoes. In the US, since 1933, That is an acceptable practice. Outside the US and its States, in the states, that is not acceptable. If you tried to get shoes

without paying for them in the states, you would be put in jail for stealing, but in the jurisdiction of the US, you

can get possession of the shoes by giving the merchant debt paper. You just can't get title. If you want the title,

you will have to give the merchant a real asset from the private side (substance). The only substance that is

yours is your exemption. That equates to credit in admiralty and equity.

March 9, 1933 73rd Congress

MR PATMAN: "Under the new law the money is issued to the banks in return for Government obligations,

bills of exchange drafts, notes, trade acceptances, and banker's acceptances. The money will be worth

100cents on the dollar, because it is backed by the credit of the Nation. It will represent a mortgage on all the

homes and other property of all the people in the Nation."

MR PATMAN: "The money so issued will not have one penny of gold coverage behind it, because it is really not

needed."

CREDITORS AND THEIR BONDS PLUS THE HIDDEN COMMERCIAL COURT PROCESS

The bills of exchange are government obligations and to the private investors.

The banker's acceptances are government obligations. When you accept a presentment for value and

sign it, you have just done a banker's acceptance. Public banks can also do a banker's acceptance. It is not designated to just one side or the other.

Have you asked who is ISSUING the new money to the banks? Can the Government issue money to the

banks? Can other banks issue money to the banks? Where is this new money that is going to be issued to

banks? Where does the bank go when it wants to be issued more money? The people have been always been

private bankers in the states in America. Now we also have public bankers. The people used to dig the gold and

silver out of the ground, have it minted, and then put it into circulation. Now the people sign notes, and give

them to the banks to turn into "debt money", and the banks put the debt into circulation "as money". It would be

against the law for the people to do that. They have to issue their credit (money) to the bank to do through the

straw men. When you use the US bond (even though it is an implied bond), to discharge a public debt, the debt

is discharged. House Joint Resolution 192 is the written public (insurance) policy guaranteeing this can be done.

The people are still issuing new money to the banks by signing notes and giving them to the banks.

Implied: This word is used in law in contrast to "express";i.e., where the intention in regard to the

subject matter is not manifested by explicit and direct words, but is gathered by implication or necessary

action from the circumstances, the general language, or the conduct of the parties.

Using the bond (debt) to discharge another debt is common in the US. Mr. Patman said the new money

represented a mortgage on all the homes and other property of all the people in the Nation. He used the word nation" with an expansive intent. There were and are no people in the nation. The nation is a political creation.

But, there are people behind all the straw men, which are in the nation. On a mortgage there is always a debtor

and a creditor. The new money was issued based on the people and US corporations turning in their gold. The

corporations were controlled by the US, but the people were not. The corporations had no substance, but the

people did. The people volunteered to enter an implied contract with the US. The New Deal was announced in

Congress in March 1933. The executive order was given in April. The gold had to be deposited in the Federal

Reserve Banks by May 1. The congress proclaimed its public policy in House Joint resolution 192 in June. The

new public policy was that no creditor on this new mortgage could require payment in any particular form of US

coin or currency. As creditors, the people could not require payment for any new mortgage in gold. Neither

could any other creditor. That New Deal made the people who participated in the salvation of the US

corporation, creditors. It also made debtors of the US corporations their officers, agents, and employee –

including all the straw men.

This is an example of set-off and adjustment of mutual debts. The straw man owes debt to a US corporation

agency, and the US owes a debt through an implied promise to the man. The US can never pay the man,

because there is no money, but the US can give the straw man debt money it can use in commerce in the US to use to get possession of products and services for you. You get to use the products or services. When you use

a bond to discharge a public debt, you have used your exemption (credit), which is the only title you can have on

the private side. You are an investor in the US corporations. That does not make you an owner. It makes you a

creditor.

CREDITORS AND THEIR BONDS PLUS THE HIDDEN COMMERCIAL COURT PROCESS

Appearance bond

This is a bond that assures you will appear in a court proceeding. It is not a catchall bond that covers everything that will come up in the case. To get the appearance bond you have to give your word (bond) that you will

appear to finish settling the accounting. It is issued by the hearing officer, if it is requested and if there is no

controversy. If you are honorable enough not to start arguing with the hearing officer or the Complainant, or the

prosecuting attorney, you can get this bond.

There must be no controversy. That fact is established by your voluntary act of accepting the charging

Instrument for value and returning it. In doing so, you are exchanging your exemption (credit) for the discharge

of the charge(s). You are bonding your pledge to appear and settle. If it were not voluntary, that would be

bondage. You must tell the hearing officer that you are not disputing any of the facts.

Dispute: A conflict or controversy; an assertion of a right, claim, or demand on one side, met by contrary

claims or allegations on the other. The subject of litigation; the matter for which a suit is brought and upon which

issue us joined, and in relation to which jurors are called and witnesses examined.

When you enter a dispute, you join the issue and confirm the existence of what was just an idea, making it

materialize and give subject matter that can be tested by a jury or witnesses.

Once you ask for the bond, it is yours. If you ask for it again, it will appear that you do not know you already have it, and the hearing officer will proceed as though he is talking to a debtor/straw man. A debtor/straw man

does not automatically get an appearance bond. It may be required to pay for a bail bond. An appearance bond

with conditions incorporates a cost to you.

If you have requested the appearance bond at no cost to you, there will be no conditions to the release. If

you do not ask for it that way, there may be conditions – like drug testing, required meetings with court

officers, or required daily or weekly phone calls. Those are a cost to you, as they take your time and your

property.

If you don't appear AND settle the accounting, you will be in dishonor of your word (your bond), and the

appearance bond will be revoked. They will not tell you it has been revoked. Your dishonor will then be

used to carry out the presumption that you are representing the straw man in a fiduciary capacity, and that

you are in breach of your fiduciary duty. That is not allowed in equity. Then the debt of the straw man will be put

on you. If there is not enough property held in the name of the straw man to cover the dishonor, or if

you as trustee refuse to turn over the trust property to settle the debt. They will take your body as surety for

the debt. It is the trustee's body being taken. You volunteered to be the trustee.

Charging order: A statutorily created means for a creditor [Plaintiff] of a judgment debtor

[Defendant] who is a partner of others [you] to reach the debtor's beneficial interest in the partnership [your

Credit], without risking dissolution of the partnership. Uniform Partnership Act, ss 28.

The purpose of the court case is for the judge to test the facts of an accounting. He is the auditor in a

possible dispute between a creditor and a debtor. The creditor always wins. It is a matter of how much the

debtor will pay that is being determined in a court case.

Audit: Systematic inspection of accounting records involving analysis, tests, and confirmations. The

hearing and investigation had before an auditor. A formal or official examination and authentication of

accounts, with witness, vouchers, etc. [L audit he hears, a hearing, from audio – to hear]

CREDITORS AND THEIR BONDS PLUS THE HIDDEN COMMERCIAL COURT PROCESS

Auditor: An officer of the court, assigned to state the items of debit and credit between the parties in

a suite where accounts are in question, and exhibit the balance. Under Rules of Civil Procedure in many

states, the term "master" is used to describe those persons formerly known as auditors;

Magistrate: [L. magister – a master, from magia - sorcery, from Greek mageia – the theology of

Magicians]

Vouch: To give personal assurance or serve as a guarantee.

Voucher: A receipt, acquittance, or release, which may serve as evidence of payment or discharge of

a debt, or to certify the correctness of accounts.

4) Surety bond

The surety bond is used to subrogate liability from one party to another. It is similar to an indemnity bond.

you can issue a surety bond to relieve someone, who is in dishonor, of potential financial damage. You can

indemnify an honorable party who may have made a mistake, by volunteering to b e his surety. This is often

the case with a judge. If you do this, you are moving into a creditor position because you are taking

responsibility for the actions of another. Three parties are requested; 1) the one who is volunteering to be the

surety, 2) the debtor, and 3) the creditor. There can be more than one creditor and more than one debtor.

Creditor status can change during the case. When you become the creditor, someone has to be the debtor,

the prosecuting attorney signed the complaint, and there is not bond in the case file, and there is no signed

security agreement, he is going to be the debtor. If he acts honorably and tells the judge he wants to settle or have the case dismissed, he stays in honor. You may have to authorize him to sign the check to settle the

accounting. If he acts in dishonor, he is the one who will be left holding the bag. You can bond the parties

and/or bond the case. [See 6 Case Bond]

Suretyship: The relationship among three parties whereby one person (the surety) [you] guarantees

payment of debtor's [Defendant] debt owed to a creditor [Plaintiff] or acts as a co-debtor [co-defendant].

generally speaking, "the relation which exists where one person [you] has undertaken an obligation, and another

person [Defendant] is also under an obligation or other duty [to give energy/credit] to the oblige [Plaintiff], who is

entitled to but one performance, and as between the two who are bound [you and the Defendant], one rather

than the other should perform."

Suretyship bond: A contractual arrangement [created by your mother's signature on the application

for the birth certificate] between the surety [you], the principal [Defendant] and the oblige [Plaintiff] whereby the

surety [you] agrees to protect the oblige [Plaintiff] if the principal {Defendant] defaults in performing the principal's

contractual obligations [discharging debt, or in anyway dishonors the Plaintiff]. The bond [your written word] is

the instrument which binds the surety [you].

The surety bond is delivered to the one who dishonored you. It is wise to have evidence of the dishonor before you issue a surety bond. Satisfactory evidence could be a certificate from a notary after an administrative

process has been completed to assure there really is a dishonor. You might just think you were dishonored.

If you are in dishonor yourself, and have not corrected the mistake, you are not in a position to be claiming you

have been dishonored. This is a very narrow window. You must always approach equity with clean hands.

The surety bond is also delivered to the bonding company if the one in dishonor is a public officer with a bond. It

is also delivered to the clerk of court, if there is a court case in process. Always get a certified copy of the surety

bond from the clerk after it is filed.

6) Case bond

CREDITORS AND THEIR BONDS PLUS THE HIDDEN COMMERCIAL COURT PROCESS

This bond is in the nature of a replevin bond. A replevin bond was formerly used in common law (equity) when

there was a dispute and one party chose to file a claim in court against another party in possession of property in

dispute. The moving party was required to bond his charge (claim) before he could get temporary possession of the subject property. The replevin bond was double the value of the subject property. Part of it was to indemnify

the sheriff who seized the subject property from the defendant in possession. The order part was to guarantee

the defendant would be reimbursed at least for the value of the seized property if it were not returned to him in

the event he won the case.

In equity all charges need to be bonded. You have heard: "Put your money where your mouth is." That is what

is happening when charges are brought in court and the moving party bonds the case. This policy assures the

defendant will not be damaged by a unsupported complaint. Charges are rarely bonded in modern court

procedures, until after the case is decided. By that time, the defendant is almost always in dishonor, so the

prosecuting attorney can use the defendant's dishonor to bond the case. It is really the defendant's

representative that is bonding the case. Again it is the man's credit that gives life to the bond. If the defendant is

in dishonor because of what its representative (trustee) said or did or did not say or did not do, it is the trustee's

credit that is used to satisfy the debt – discharge the bond.

You can voluntarily bond the case if there is no bond already in the clerk's file. Be sure to get a certified copy of

the docket sheet as evidence there is no bond in the case, before you issue your bond. When you Bond the case, you are the creditor and creditors win. If you bond the case, become the creditor, and then dishonor the

judge, the attorneys, or the process in any way, you will lose your position as a creditor and go back to

representing the defendant. All the dishonors are pinned on the defendant even if you are the one who went into

dishonor through your words or your actions. The defendant cannot talk or act. It all comes from you.

If you bond the case and underwrite all the obligations/loss/cost/ of the honorable citizens of the State of

_____, that would include the attorney, as long he is honorable. If he is not, he refuses the

Indemnification and volunteers to have his dishonor give the commercial energy to the settlement. It is up to

him. The judge will go along with what he requests. Usually, the attorney will tell the judge that the

Plaintiff moves for dismissal.

7) Performance bond

Performance bonds guarantee that parties to a contract will not be damaged by the conduct or lack of conduct of

an officer. This could include an executor, trustee, officer of a court, officer of a corporation, guardian,

etc. Wherever there is a fiduciary duty, there may be a need for a performance bond. An oath is a performance

bond in common law. In the modern States and integrated court system, bonds are backed by

insurance companies. They are actually insurance policies.

Performance bond: Type of contract bond, which protects against loss due to the inability or refusal

of a contractor to perform his contract. Such are normally required on public construction projects.

Official bond: A bond given by a public officer, conditioned that he shall well and faithfully

perform all the duties of the office.

Contractor: One who in pursuit of independent business undertakes to perform a job or piece of

Work, retaining in himself control of means, method and manner of accomplishing the desired result.

Construction: Interpretation of statute, regulation, court decision or other legal authority. The

process, or the art, of determining the sense, real meaning, or proper explanation of obscure, complex or

ambiguous terms or provision in a statute, written instrument, or oral agreement, or the application of such

subject to the case in question, by reasoning in the light derived from extraneous connected circumstances or

CREDITORS AND THEIR BONDS PLUS THE HIDDEN COMMERCIAL COURT PROCESS

actions or writings bearing upon the same or a connected matter. Or by seeking and applying the probably aim or purpose of the provision. Drawing conclusions respecting subjects that lie beyond the direct expression of

the term.

Refusal: The act of one who has, by law, a right and power of having or doing something of

advantage, and declines it. ...a refusal implies the positive denial of an application or command, or at least

evidential determination not to comply.

Power: Authority to do any act which the grantor (you) might himself lawfully perform.

The following is taken from In Search of Liberty in America (one of Byron's books)

Why do officers of government hold positions called "trust or profit"? Look at some constitutions to find the

phrase. References to the Constitution for the Unites States of America are provided below.

Any Office of honor, Trust or Profit under the United States" Article I, Section 3

Any Office of honor, Trust or Profit under the United States" Article I, Section 9

Any Senator or Representative, or Person holding an Office of Trust or Profit under the United

States" Article II, section 1

Any Office or public Trust under the United States" Article VI, clause 3

Suffice it to say, trillions of dollars in assets are being held in these Trusts in America today. You can verify this if you study the Comprehensive Annual Financial Reports that each corporate entity within the

Unites States empire is required to have.

The Trust transfers possession of trust assets to another, the trustee can make rules and regulations for the use

of the Trust property and also rules for the conduct of those "persons" accepting protection or receiving

property. Trust property may remain in the so-called public forum held directly by the Trust or its partners or

corporations, or it may be conveyed into the private domain. It is all effectively Trust property,

public and private, until it is taken out of the protection of Trust.

CREDITORS AND THEIR BONDS PLUS THE HIDDEN COMMERCIAL COURT PROCESS

RULES OF THE GAME

RULE #1: The fiction and real cannot mix. The public and the private cannot mix.

You cannot create a public debt.

That is against the law.

A creditor can issue a bond (evidence of a public debt) and use the bond to discharge other public debts.

You cannot use the public federal reserve routing numbers on the private credit instruments you issue.

Those routing numbers are public.

Your credit instruments use your private routing number (EIN) with the closed account number.

You are a private banker.

The closed account number was accepted and put on a UCC-1.

Your acceptance of the account number takes it to the private side for adjustment and setoff.

You gave notice to John Snow, or his predecessor, that you had accepted the account as collateral.

Your secured party collateral rights are private.

You are a secured party on the private side even without filing a UCC-1

The UCC-1 is to give notice on the public side of your collateral rights.

That is why you can use the account for adjustment and setoff of public debts.

There is no money on the private side.

Debt is used on the public side to discharge other public debts.

There is no money on the public side either, but debt is accepted "as money".

The debts that are owed to you by the public, can be used to discharge public debts.

A debt is a liability to the debtor and an asset, a bond, each time you use your credit.

You can bond your bill of exchange, or use a bond.

Either way, it is a bond (evidence of a public debt owed to you) that discharges the public debt.

If the State cannot file a claim against you, because it is a fictitious entity and you are a real man, then it

must file a claim against s straw man to get to you. What is it trying to get? Does it want your body in jail?

The money in your bank account? Your house? Your business?

The answer is NO. It wants your credit. It already has the rest of it, because everything is either registered

or found on registered property. The state does not want the things that are held in the name of the straw

man, but it has no compunction against taking those things, if you dishonor it in any way. All those things,

except your body, belong to the straw man, which is an officer, agent, or employee of the US or one of its

States. They do not belong to you. The "money" (FRN's) belongs to the Federal Reserve, because it is the

entity that created it. The straw man just gets to use it as long as if follows the federal reserve rules. The

title to the real property associated with your house is held by the straw man. The business license for your

business was issued to the straw man. The registration for the car names the straw man as the owner. The

driver's license was issued to the straw man. None of those assets belong to you. They are all pieces of

paper that belong to the straw man, UNLESS it fails to follow the rules.

CREDITORS AND THEIR BONDS PLUS THE HIDDEN COMMERCIAL COURT PROCESS

Presentment has a complaint – a moving party. What is it trying to move? What is its complaint? It

Is usually using a statute as the grounds for the complaint. If public and private can't mix, the complaint

Must be against the public straw man – not you. Why would the State care if a piece of paper violated a

(fictitious) law? What is the motivation?

State is trying to move you to let it use your credit. If you refuse, the State can move the court to grant

the use from your dishonor. Does the State really have a complaint, or is it just asking for your help? Maybe

the complaint is that it is out of "money". There is no money. None on the private side (gold and silver).

None on the public side (except your credit).

Does the office manager do when it needs more money for paperclips? It requisitions the guys on the top floor

for money to buy more paperclips. Do the bosses say, "No Way!"? Of course not! That would be

counter-productive to the purpose of the business. Think of the State as your business. You need to be sure

there are enough paperclips, or the business may fail. Why would you refuse to honor the requisition? Why

you argue about whether or not the requisition form was filled out properly? Why would you deny

you are the proper party to fulfill the requisition? Why would you ignore the requisition? Why would get mad and start charging the messenger with fraud? If you ignore the requisitions and spend all your

boss's money trying not to fulfill the requisitions, the business will fail. Where would that leave you?

Your business is down the tubes. You might be in jail for breach of contract. Your property has been taken

by the corporate attorneys. Your money is gone. All the people who depended on your business have to use

other sources of your products and services. You are a very irresponsible business man. If you had just

signed the requisition, you would still be on the top floor. Instead, the trust assets are gone and you are

making license plates.

The State has no substance. It has no money. It has no inherent right to anything, except what it has created

which is the straw man. It has a very important function. It has been charged with providing for the means by

Which you can go into grocery stores, gas stations, libraries, shopping malls, airports, car dealerships, and

marts. It is does not get "money" from somewhere, it cannot continue to provide the infrastructure you

find so convenient. The only source it has is taxes. License, permit, and registration fees are a source of

revenue for the State, but that is not sufficient for the giant octopus feeding machine we have grown to love

and depend on. It needs to feed off your credit, and if you don't voluntarily let the State use it, the State will use your dishonor to take it.

CREDITORS AND THEIR BONDS PLUS THE HIDDEN COMMERCIAL COURT PROCESS

If you have filed a claim against the straw man, the State doesn't even control that anymore. If you have

named the Secretary of State as the secured party, it has additional expenses as trustee of the property held in

the name of that straw man. The situation is getting worse for the State. Where will it get the money it

needs to continue supplying all the services you expect from it? It has to go to you and ask you for your

credit.

Have you ever had to ask your dad for financial help after you left his house and were out on your own? It is

embarrassing! The State does not want to just ask if it can use your credit. It will have to find creative ways

to ask for it, get it, and save face in the process.

The trick is for the State to ask for your help without the un-enlightened person/US citizens being able to

see it. The State must have your credit, AND it is going to get it one way or the other. It is going to get it

the easy way or the hard way. It is all up to you.

So the only thing the State can't take is your body and other substance in your possession, UNLESS you voluntarily authorized the State to use it. You always have a choice to retain possession of your substance,

or let the State take possession of it. Remember, possession is 9/10 of the law. What is the other 1/10 then?

HONOR

RULE #2: Stay in honor at all costs.

Your mission should you decide to accept it, is to honor the State when it asks you (in its aggressive way), to

let it use your credit (exemption). The State is raising you up as a creditor every time it gives you a

presentment. It is your choice. You can honor the State by accepting its presentment and issuing an

authorization VOLUNTARILY for it to get enough of your credits to equal the value of its presentment –

dollar for dollar, OR You can VOLUNTARILY dishonor the State by refusing, arguing, making it prove its

claim, or defending the straw man, pretending the State has no right to make its claim.

Wow! That is a hard choice, You can voluntarily authorize the State's use of your exemption, or you can

voluntarily dishonor the State, at which time it will use your dishonor to take property from the straw man or take

your body and collect rent while you sit in jail. Gee- What should I do? What should I do?

CREDITORS AND THEIR BONDS PLUS THE HIDDEN COMMERCIAL COURT PROCESS

There is an easy way and a hard way. The choice is always yours. The State is only following your lead. If you

argue or defend, it gets to use your exemption AND maybe take some of your possessions besides. If you

accept and authorize the State to use your exemption, it is required to accept it. What do you have to lose? Is

your exemption limited? Can it be depleted? No! What difference does it make if the State gets to use your

exemption? The difference is, the grocery stores and Wal-Mart's stay open. The fire department responds to fire

calls. The garbage trucks pick up your garbage, and the streets are repaired.

When you understand how to stay in honor, it is a win / win situation. If you do not know how to stay in honor,

It might be a win / lose situation, with you losing. The State will get what it wants either way.

RULE #3: there is no money.

What do you use to pay your bills? If there is no money, what does the State use to pay its bills? Do you

really have any bills? Who's name is on the contract with the electric company, the mortgage, the credit card, or

the student loan? It isn't your name. It is the straw man's name.

The constitution says ... no state shall make anything but gold or silver coin a tender in payment of debts.

Well, there it is – a prohibition against the states. Does it say the United States or its agents can't use something other than gold or silver for payment of debts? No! Since there is no gold or silver coin in circulation

in the United States, and all the businesses you have grown to love are in the United States, it is a

good thing the United States has created a straw man for you to control and federal reserve notes for it to use

or you would use money, if you had some.

The Straw man is able to pay all its bills with federal reserve notes. You can't, but the straw man can. Isn't

It neat that you control a straw man/person? The trouble is – the straw man can't get a real title to anything

with federal reserve notes. You can get possession of the substance, but you only get to retain

possession as long as you stay in honor. The straw man stays in equity honor, and you fulfill your fiduciary

duties as the presumed trustee. If you choose to go into dishonor , you voluntarily give up possession of

whatever property the State wants to take to get the credits it needs to keep its business ventures going.

nothing personal – Just business!

CREDITORS AND THEIR BONDS PLUS THE HIDDEN COMMERCIAL COURT PROCESS

RULE #5: Do not participate in public plays.

When the state invites the straw man to participate in one of its revenue events, you have options. The

Presumption is that you will volunteer to represent the accused straw man. They are pretty sure you will do

That because you always have before. Think of the event as a play. The play has actors with scripts. Each

Actor knows the plot, his lines, and the outcome. Their play has been practiced over and over in every county

In every state. The outcome is almost always the same. A man (not one of the scheduled actors) crashes into

Their party, and carries out the plot. Without the man, the whole plot changes, The outcome changes, They

Need the man to get the same ending as they always have before. When the man does not participate in their

play, there is confusion and chaos. The planned script does not work without the man.

The usual scenario includes the man volunteering to represent the accused straw man, as a trustee. Each time

a straw man is charged a new trust is created. It is even possible that each time the straw man's name is

spelled in a slightly different way in the complaining presentment, a different trust is created. There might

be 2 or 4 different trusts referenced in the same presentment. Each trust is going to produce income for the

plaintiff, if the script is followed as planned.

It all has to do with trusts.

Everywhere you look, there are trusts. The straw man is a trust when it is named on a complaint, indictment,

or traffic ticket. Sometimes it is a cestu que trust when it is the beneficiary of another trust. Sometimes it is

the trustor or another trust. Sometimes it is a corporation sole. Sometimes it is a defendant. Sometimes it is

a plaintiff. Sometimes it is a debtor. Sometimes it is a creditor. Sometimes it is a secured party. It is a very

versatile vehicle or tool.

There are always at least three parties to a trust. No one OWNs a trust on the private side; but on the public

side, there is always a "responsible party", who is deemed to be the owner to the trust. This is a fallacy that

is often used by the State in relation to trusts that have real property as the trust corpus. They always want to

know who the owner of the trust is. A trust is just an agreement among three or more parties. The trustee

holds the legal title to the trust corpus, and is the one deemed to be owner of the public trust. It is useless

to argue with public property or is involved with federal reserve notes, it qualifies as a public trust. The

beneficiary holds the equitable title to the trust corpus. The title is bifurcated.

CREDITORS AND THEIR BONDS PLUS THE HIDDEN COMMERCIAL COURT PROCESS

Trust: A legal entity created by a grantor for the benefit of designated beneficiaries under the laws of

the state and the valid trust instrument.

Indenture: The document which contains the terms and conditions which govern the conduct of the

trustee and the rights of the beneficiaries.

Exchanger: (exchange) to part with, give or transfer for an equivalent.

Trustor: One who creates a trust. Also called settlor.

Settlor: The grantor or donor in a deed of settlement. Also, one who creates a trust.

Trust corpus: [trust property] the property which is the subject matter of the trust. The trust res.

Creator: One who creates.

Trustee: Person holding property in trust. One who holds legal title to property "in trust" for the benefit of

another person (beneficiary) and who must carry out specific duties with regard to the property.

Legal title: One which is complete and perfect so far as regards the apparent right of ownership and

possession, but which carries no beneficial interest in the property, another person being equitably entitled

thereto.

Beneficiary: One who benefits from act of another.

Equitable title: A right in the party to whom it belongs to have the legal title transferred to him, or the beneficial interest of one person whom equity regards as the real owner.

Surety: A person who is primarily liable for payment of debt or performance of obligation of another.

Creditor: One to whom money is due, and, in ordinary acceptation, has reference to financial or

business transctions.

The original straw man trust, Mom was the Exchanger / Trustor / Settlor

Mother applied to the State of_____for the creation of a trust. She chose the date of birth for it.

She chose its name. She requested evidence that it had been created = a birth certificate. She was the

Informant. She delivered the paper description of the original property to the trust Creator. It was a

description of the real substance. The paper description was the original trust corpus. More trust property

be added later.

State of_____was the Creator of the original trust.

State complied with mom's request and created a straw man with the name and date of birth your mother

requested. She applied for a Social Security number for it. She put it into commerce by getting it medical

numbers, a day care center matriculation number, a public school matriculation number, a little league ID

number, a library card number, etc., etc., etc. Sometimes the Creator is also the original Exchanger, Trustor,

Settlor.

CREDITORS AND THEIR BONDS PLUS THE HIDDEN COMMERCIAL COURT PROCESS

Who is the beneficiary of the original trust?

The beneficiary changes each time a new trust is created. You re the original beneficiary though, If you

choose to use your beneficial interest. If you choose not to use it, the citizens of the state that created it are

the beneficiaries. This is part of the Highest and Best Use principle. If the property is not being put to its highest

and best use, it can be "borrowed" for a time and put to better use. You have not been using it. You have not

filed any claims against it, so why should it just sit there not being used? This first trust was

created for your benefit, it you choose to use it. Remember, the reason the first party (creator) creates a trust, is

for the second party (trustee) to manage the trust corpus for the benefit of a third party (beneficiary).

What is the trust corpus?

The State complied with mom's request and created a straw man with the name and date of birth she requested.

Mom is the one who put your physical description on the application for the certificate / evidence that the trust had been created. She "delivered" the description (7 pounds 11 ounces, 19 1/2 inches long, and a

footprint). All of this was on paper. The paper is the trust corpus. That was the consideration that was

exchanged into the original trust. Exchanged for what? --- the ability to gain possession (not title) of houses,

cars, shoes, books, etc. without paying for them.

She applied for a Social Security number for it. She put it into commerce by getting it medical records, a day

care center matriculation number, a public school matriculation number, a league ID number, a library card, etc.,

etc., etc. All of these paper contracts between the trust and agencies of municipal corporations are trust assets.

These are all part of the trust corpus – the trust property. They are all property that can be used

as evidence to contractual obligations the trust has OR as collateral for debts the trust owns. It appears the trust

is using your description and your credit to gain assets. It has an obligation to you. Maybe these assets can be

considered benefits for which you owe an obligation because of your close relationship with the trust, OR these

assets can be considered collateral for the debt the trust owes to you.

Who is the trustee?

On the private side, if an appointed trustee resigns or dies, the trust corpus reverts to the beneficiaries or back to

the trustor. It is useless to create a trust without appointing a trustee. The trustee created by the state upon mom's request must also have a trustee. The problem is, depending on how it is going to be used; the

creation of the trust is a matter of construction and operation of law. This is constructive trust.

Constructive trust: Trust created by operation of law against one who by actual or constructive

fraud, by duress or by abuse or confidence, or by commission of wrong, or by any form of

unconscionable conduct, or other questionable means, has obtained or holds legal right to property

which he should not, in equity and good conscience, hold and enjoy.

CREDITORS AND THEIR BONDS PLUS THE HIDDEN COMMERCIAL COURT PROCESS

Construction: Drawing conclusions respecting subjects that i.e. beyond the direct expression of the

term.

Operation of law: This term expresses the manner in which rights, and sometimes liabilities, devolve

upon a person by the mere application to the particular transaction of the established rules of law,

without the act or co-operation of the party himself.

Default: An omission of that which ought to be done. Specifically, the omission or failure to perform a

legal or contractual duty.

There can be more than one trustee for a trust. One trustee may have the duty of performing certain

actions of the trust. Another trustee may perform different functions. The identity of the trustee or

trustees of these "individual" trusts is often not expressed, as there is no requirement for there to even be a

written trust indenture. On the public side, there must always be a default trustee, if no one volunteers to

fill the duties of the trustee. When a corporation or limited liability company is created, the statutory

default managing is the Secretary of State of the state where the entity is being created. In some

States the SOS would be the logical default trustee. In other cases, the lack of a trustee may result in a

presumption that you re the trustee.,

Trustees have a fiduciary duty to manage the trust honorably and for the benefit of the beneficiary. A trustee may

not use the trust for personal gain. A trustee that is acting outside his duty or not performing at all is in

breach of his fiduciary duty. That is not tolerated on the private side or the public side. Trustees in breach of

fiduciary duty are held personally responsible for the breach and take on the financial penalties for their

actions (malfeasance) or lack of action (nonfeasance).

Here is an example of a typical court scenario when a man participates:

Investigator from ABC agency or a municipal corporation has filed an information with a prosecuting attorney. On the public side, affidavits are not required. The informant is not required to sign an affidavit submit it

to the attorney to commence a public action against the individual being investigated.

Affidavits were required in equity when someone wanted to file a claim in court. In admiralty in the public

affidavits are no longer required. They have been replaced with what is called an information. An

affidavit is signed under oath. The statements made in an affidavit are the signor's bond. His word is his bond.

The affidavit formerly bonded the case. Now that there are no affidavits, there are no bonds to bond

cases.

The prosecuting attorney has to decide whether or not to commence an action. The informant may have

completed an administrative process (IRS –m 90 day letter, 30 day letter, 10 day letter) for the attorney

as the basis for bringing the action. It may not have started an administrative process. Nine

CREDITORS AND THEIR BONDS PLUS THE HIDDEN
COMMERCIAL COURT PROCESS

times out of ten, the administrative process is not needed, because they are almost sure you will agree

(without knowing it) to represent the accused individual (the trust) by volunteering to act as its trustee. The

Attorney is going to create a new trust to be the accused on the complaint or indictment. If you go into contempt

for defending and not taking responsibility for the new trust, you will either pay with the trust

Corpus, OR you will go to jail, and your credit (exemption) will be tapped during the time they are housing and

feeding you and giving you medical treatment. The trust corpus might include the balance in a bank

Account, a title to real property or a car, or any other public asset.

Creator

The attorney is the creator of the accused trust. It might be JOHN HENRY DOE. Notice that they never put your

name on a complaint, indictment, or traffic ticket. Even if it is written in upper case and lower case

Letters, it is still a fiction and a trust. We cannot mix public and private.

Trust name

The name of the trust is JOHN HENRY DOE. In the body of the complaint, a reference may be made to

JOHN HENRY DOE or JOHN DOE or John Doe. This is how the judgment can be multiplied. These might all be

new trusts against which the final judgment can be applied, and for which it is presumed you will volunteer

to be the trustee, and through which you will be presumed to be surety. The trust is expected to be the

defendant. The question is --- who is the trustee and who is taking responsibility for the trust activities?

Trustor

The attorney is also the trustor. He is putting the trust corpus into the trust. That is the charge. It is a debt (liability) on the public side, and a credit (asset) on the private side. We have always presumed a charge is

a bad thing. It is only bad if the man is found in contempt of the process, or of the attorney, or of the judge,

or of a number of other possibilities. It is very easy to go into contempt. If you don't agree to take

responsibility, you will be in contempt of our presumed fiduciary duty. Creditors do not go into contempt.

Beneficiary

The beneficiary is the State of_____, which is also the plaintiff in this case. It is the person that stands to

gain from the charges (trust corpus), but it only has the equitable interest in the trust corpus. That way, the

beneficiary is not help responsible for bringing a claim without a bond (evidence of a debt). The attorney

does it instead. The beneficiary has to hold onto its creditor position, and can't if it brings unfounded claims.

The plaintiff seldom signs the complaint. The attorney's signature is usually the only one on it.

Trustee

This the trust position that carries all the liability. The trustee has a fiduciary duty to manage this trust

property for the benefit of the State of_____,. It it does not, the trustee accepts the responsibility for the

losses suffered by the beneficiary, the State.

there is no appointed trustee. There is a presumption that there will be a trustee when it is needed. The

attorney has the complaint served on the original trust with a name like the accused individual (the defendant

trust). Someone has to represent the defendant.

At this point the only representative for the trust is its creator, the prosecuting attorney. Which has made a

commitment to the beneficiary. Once the charge is signed by the attorney and delivered to someone who

might volunteer to be the trustee, the attorney does not even have the option of withdrawing the charge

without the defendant's agreement (Rule of Court). Since the complaint was delivered into your hands, as

the presumed trustee and surety, you have to agree to the withdrawal of the charges before they can be

withdrawn.

CREDITORS AND THEIR BONDS PLUS THE HIDDEN COMMERCIAL COURT PROCESS

soon as you hire a good attorney or decide to defend the trust yourself, the liability has moved from the

prosecuting attorney to you. The fact that you are defending, all by itself, is a dishonor. Anything other than

all-out acceptance is a dishonor. Your dishonor is what gives the prosecuting attorney the energy to bond the

case. All cases have to be bonded. Whoever bonds the case is the creditor. Whoever is in dishonor is the

debtor. They need you to dishonor the process, the attorneys, or the judge to have the standard script result

the standard outcome. If you fail to immediately go into dishonor, there will be plenty of opportunities in the

script for you to carry out the plot to get you into dishonor.

You can plead Not Guilty, testify, defend, call witnesses, question witnesses, file motions, file a counter suit, answer questions, or not respond at all --- just to name a few ways to volunteer to be the trustee and to be in

Honor. Your voluntary dishonor will authorize the use of your credit to bond the case. Since you did not

voluntarily bond the case, you are in dishonor.

Surety

Since the standard script will be used for the court event, it is likely the man who has volunteered to be the

trustee for the accused trust, will defend the trust. That will guarantee the standard outcome. The defendant will

be found guilty and the trust corpus will be liquidated enough to "pay" the judgment debt. If the event

involves criminal charges, the man's body will be jailed so the state can RE-VENUE the man's credit from private

into the public state. This is what keeps the public machine running. REVENUE. The man will

be the surety for the judgment debtor once the trust is found guilty.

Plaintiff

State (beneficiary) is the plaintiff and presumed creditor, as long as the man plays by the standard script.

Defendant

The prosecuting attorney needs to have a volunteer to defend the trust, or he will be stuck representing the

accused trust himself. He is the defendant, but does not plan on holding the position very long. With the

help of the judge and the defense attorney, the prosecuting attorney will be able to pass the liability on to the

trust and its representative and surety – you – but you have to go into dishonor for this to happen.

All charges, arguments, and testimony is dangerous in the public court.

Remember it is not your court. They can only see fictions, so if you are testifying, you are recognized only as a

fiction as you are a piece of paper, but if you are talking to him, he presumes you are the trustee for the trust

er). In that capacity, he can talk to you. He is expecting you to breach your fiduciary duties by going

into dishonor. Then they win – you lose. You want a win / win situation.

Be careful even with the copyright. If you can bring the copyright into the case without testifying (through third

party witnesses), you may be able to stave off a demand for trust property. If you have already given

The right to use the now-copyrighted name to a corporation, you cannot revoke it that authorization after the fact.

You may have done that by applying for a loan. You gave them the use of the name on the

application. You can give the use of the name on a driver's license application. You are the one who tells

what name to put on the license. You can't come back later and charge them for using the name you

previously gave them. If there is no driver's license application, you my be able to give notice of the

copyright to the officer, and then enforce the copyright violation because he had notice of your restrictions to

use of the name. Even if the car is registered with the State, you may be able to use the copyright in this

action, if you know how and do not dishonor your own claim to being the private owner of the name.

CREDITORS AND THEIR BONDS PLUS THE HIDDEN COMMERCIAL COURT PROCESS

Here is a different scenario when the man does NOT participate:

An investigator from ABC agency of a municipal corporation has filed an information with a prosecuting

attorney. Before things get this far, you should have completed your administrative procedure on the

activity that is the subject matter of the court case. [See the section on Administrative Process]

The prosecuting attorney has decided to commence an action. The attorney creates a new trust to be the

accused on the complaint or indictment, which is delivered into your hands.

This time you accept the presentment for value, return it, and authorize the use of your credit, and bond the

case. You give notice to the public of these private actions you have taken. You use third parties to testify

to the agreement of the parties of the dishonor of the plaintiff, if necessary. You do not get involved in the issues

of the case other than the agreement of the parties. You can bond the case. You do not have to be the

trustee and represent the accused trust to take responsibility for the presumed violations of the State's statutes.

You are one of the people. You are a creditor with priority over fictions. You are the One – the One who

has the power to create a Win / Win situation for all parties.

Creator

The prosecuting attorney is still the creator.

Trust name

The name of the trust is still JOHN HENRY DOE.

Trustor

The prosecuting attorney is still putting the charge into the trust as a corpus.

Beneficiary

The beneficiary is still the State of_____.

Trustee

Since you have not volunteered to be the trustee, the prosecuting attorney is still the responsible party. You are

the one who accepted delivery of the complaint that was sent to the trust over which you are presumed to

be the trustee. If you can stay in honor while you take on the obligations of the trust, by using your

exemption and your credit as surety for the trust, you will be fine. You can argue with the attorneys and the

judge and the witnesses and the clerk, showing how bad a trustee you are. Or You can accept the State's

request for revenue and authorize the use of your exemption (credit). It is your choice.

Surety

The suretyship on this case can be shared. Suretyship is a voluntary act. You can volunteer to be the surety

Using your exemption (credit). Someone else can volunteer to dishonor someone or to dishonor the process,

Thereby becoming the surety. Free will is always a factor here. The big question is --- who will be the

Surety? Since there seldom is a bond in the case until after the trial is over, you can present your bond to

Bond the case.

Plaintiff

Whoever bonds the case is the plaintiff. Charges cannot be brought unless there is a bond. If the man

Supplies the bond, the man is the creditor. The tables can turn. You can do a counterclaim by removing the case

into another court for judicial review of your administrative process and get an estoppel on their case.

Defendant

The prosecuting attorney is the defendant, unless there is a defense attorney who has put a notice of

appearance into the case. If, so, then the defense attorney is the defendant. As the creditor, you can authorize

the prosecuting attorney or defense attorney if he has filed his notice of appearance, to write the check to

Settle the account. The check is backed by your bond.

STOCK WARRANTS

STOCK WARRANTS are the options that give investors the right to buy a company's stock at a specific price until the expiration date.

FEATURES

➤ Rise in total outstanding shares
➤ Fixed prices.
➤ No voting & dividend
➤ Not usually listed on stock exchanges.

TYPES

1) **CALL WARRANT:** Represents the right to buy a certain no. of stocks
2) **PUT WARRANT:** Represents amount of stock that is sold to issuer

USEFULNESS TO ISSUER

- Increase in company's capital
- Attaching warrants with bonds makes the shares more attractive.
- Finances during bankruptcy
- Future source of capital
- Investors will to buy the shares easily.

USEFULNESS TO INVESTOR

- Lower purchase price when there is a lower price of warrant price than the stock price.
- Investors can trade warrants if he expects the prices of the underlying security to go up in future.

STOCK WARRANTS

1. Issued by the co.
2. Co. does issue new shares when a holder exercises the option.
3. Raises the capital when the co. issues new shares.
4. Usually offered at a lower price.
5. Warrants could be up to 15 years.
6. Usually traded over the counter.
7. Usually given to investors.
8. Better for tax purposes.

VS

STOCK OPTIONS

1. Not issued by the co.
2. Co. does not issue new shares when a holder exercises the option.
3. Co, doesn't get any money when stock options are purchased or sold.
4. Usually offered at a higher price.
5. Maximum duration is 2-3 years.
6. Usually publically traded.
7. Usually given to the employees.
8. Not so better for tax purposes.

Stock Warrants – Features, Types, Benefits And More

Stock Warrants are the options that give investors the right to buy a company's stock at a specific price until the expiration date. The company itself issues these options and gives investors the right (but not obligation) to buy the stock. Meaning, an investor is free to decide if he wants to buy the underlying security or not. Thus, a warrant in itself does not give the holder the ownership of the stock, rather the right to buy the stock in the future.

Stock warrants are mostly given along with the bond. When a company issues a bond, it attaches a warrant along to make it more attractive for the investors. So, warrants are a bonus for the bond investors.

What Is a Bond?

A bond is a fixed income instrument that represents a loan made by an investor to a borrower (typically corporate or governmental). A bond could be thought of as an I.O.U. between the lender and borrower that includes the details of the loan and its payments. Bonds are used by companies, municipalities, states, and sovereign governments to finance projects and operations. Owners of bonds are debtholders, or creditors, of the issuer. Bond details include the end date when the principal of the loan is due to be paid to the bond owner and usually includes the terms for variable or fixed interest payments made by the borrower.

KEY TAKEAWAYS

- Bonds are units of corporate debt issued by companies and securitized as tradeable assets.
- A bond is referred to as a fixed income instrument since bonds traditionally paid a fixed interest rate (coupon) to debtholders. Variable or floating interest rates are also now quite common.
- Bond prices are inversely correlated with interest rates: when rates go up, bond prices fall and vice-versa.
- Bonds have maturity dates at which point the principal amount must be paid back in full or risk default.

The Issuers of Bonds

Governments (at all levels) and corporations commonly use bonds in order to borrow money. Governments need to fund roads, schools, dams or other infrastructure. The sudden expense of war may also demand the need to raise funds.

Similarly, corporations will often borrow to grow their business, to buy property and equipment, to undertake profitable projects, for research and development or to hire employees. The problem that large organizations run into is that they typically need far more money than the average bank can provide. Bonds provide a solution by allowing many individual investors to assume the role of the lender. Indeed, public debt markets let thousands of investors each lend a portion of the capital needed. Moreover, markets allow lenders to sell their bonds to other investors or to buy bonds from other individuals—long after the original issuing organization raised capital.

How Bonds Work

Bonds are commonly referred to as fixed income securities and are one of three asset classes individual investors are usually familiar with, along with stocks (equities) and cash equivalents.

Many corporate and government bonds are publicly traded; others are traded only over-the-counter (OTC) or privately between the borrower and lender.

When companies or other entities need to raise money to finance new projects, maintain ongoing operations, or refinance existing debts, they may issue bonds directly to investors. The borrower (issuer) issues a bond that includes the terms of the loan, interest payments that will be made, and the time at which the loaned funds (bond principal) must be paid back (maturity date). The interest payment (the coupon) is part of the return that bondholders earn for loaning their funds to the issuer. The interest rate that determines the payment is called the coupon rate.

The initial price of most bonds is typically set at par, usually $100 or $1,000 face value per individual bond. The actual market price of a bond depends on a number of factors: the credit quality of the issuer, the length of time until expiration, and the coupon rate compared to the general interest rate environment at the time. The face value of the bond is what will be paid back to the borrower once the bond matures.

Most bonds can be sold by the initial bondholder to other investors after they have been issued. In other words, a bond investor does not have to hold a bond all the way through to its maturity date. It is also common for bonds to be repurchased by the borrower if interest rates decline, or if the borrower's credit has improved, and it can reissue new bonds at a lower cost.

In order to win in court you have to redeem the Bond. AUTOTRIS CUSIP DTCC

IT IS ALL ABOUT BONDS What they're doing in these courts is all about Bonds. When you go into the courtroom after you're arrested, they use two different sets of Bonds. What they do when your arrested they fill out a "Bid Bond". The United States District Court uses 273, 274 & 275. SF = "Standard Form". Standard Form 273, Standard Form 274 & Standard Form 275. This is the United States District

Court. There is another set of Bonds and they are all put out by GSA = General Services Administration. I'm just talking off the top of my head because I have all of this stuff memorized. GSA Form SF24 is the "Bid Bond", everyone should have a copy of the Bid Bond. The "Performance Bond" is SF25.

REINSURANCE AGREEMENT FOR A BONDS STATUTE PAYMENT BOND (See instructions on reverse)	OMB Control Number: 9000-0045 Expiration Date: 7/31/2019

Paperwork Reduction Act Statement - This information collection meets the requirements of 44 USC § 3507, as amended by section 2 of the Paperwork Reduction Act of 1995. You do not need to answer these questions unless we display a valid Office of Management and Budget (OMB) control number. The OMB control number for this collection is 9000-0045. We estimate that it will take 60 minutes to read the instructions, gather the facts, and answer the questions. Send only comments relating to our time estimate, including suggestions for reducing this burden, or any other aspects of this collection of information to: General Services Administration, Regulatory Secretariat Division (M1V1CB), 1800 F Street, NW, Washington, DC 20405.

1. DIRECT WRITING COMPANY*	1A. DATE DIRECT WRITING COMPANY EXECUTES THIS AGREEMENT
	1B. STATE OF INCORPORATION
2. REINSURING COMPANY*	2A. AMOUNT OF THIS REINSURANCE $
	2B. DATE REINSURING COMPANY EXECUTES THIS AGREEMENT
	2C. STATE OF INCORPORATION

3. DESCRIPTION OF CONTRACT	4. DESCRIPTION OF BOND
3A. AMOUNT OF CONTRACT	4A. PENAL SUM OF BOND
3B. CONTRACT DATE 3C. CONTRACT NUMBER	4B. DATE OF BOND 4C. BOND NUMBER

The "Payment Bond" is SF25A and put out by the GSA. O.K. So, what are they doing with these Bonds? What's going on in the courtroom is that they are suing you for a debt collection. If you look at these Bonds, everyone of these Bonds: the "Bid Bond", the "Performance Bond" & the "Payment Bond", all have a "PENAL SUM" attached to it. The reason for the "Penal Sum" is if you don't pay the Debt, you go into "Default Judgment". That is what is going on in the courtroom. That is why all of these guys are sitting in prison wondering what's going on! If you go in and argue jurisdiction or refuse to answer questions that the judge or the court addresses to you, they will find you in contempt of court and they will put you in jail. What they do is arrest you, then they hold you, basically until the suit has been completed. Once they get "Default Judgment" on you because of your failure to pay the Debt, they put you in prison. Theattorneys are there to create a smoke screen. What attorneys have been trained to do is to lead you into "Dishonor" or "Default Judgment". Then the court puts you into prison then they sell your

"Default Judgment". Who do they sell it to? Believe it or not, the U.S. District Court buys all of these State Court Judgments. I don't know why noone has found this out before. There are about 300 "re-insurance" companies that buy these bonds. They are all 'insurance" companies. These are the people that are buying these Bonds when you went into "Default Judgment" and they cannot buy these Bonds unless they are Certified by the Secretary of the Treasury. What are they doing with these Bonds? They have regulations governing these Bonds – there are 2,000 regulations governing these Bonds. Commercial Paper; Negotiable Instruments - anything you put your signature on is a Negotiable Instrument under the Uniform Commercial Code which is the Lex Mercantorium. Its Mercantile Civil Law. The reason they use Lex Merchantorium in the court room is because everyone of you are Merchant's at Law and Merchants at Law is anyone who holds themselves out to be an expert.

Because you use commercial paper on a daily basis, you are considered to be an 'expert'. This is also why they are not telling you what is really going on in the courtroom. You are presumed to know this stuff because you hold yourself out to be an expert by using commercial paper every day. Every time you put your signature on a piece of paper, you are creating a Negotiable Instrument. Some are Non-Negotiable and some are Negotiable. Every time you endorse something, you are acting as an accommodation party or an accommodation maker under UCC 3-419. An accommodation party is anyone who loans their signature to another party. Read UCC 3-419, it tells you what an accommodation maker is and what an accommodation party is. When you loan your signature to them, they can then re-write your signature on any document they want and that's exactly what they are doing. What the Federal Courts are doing is they are buying up these state court default judgments, called 'criminal cases' to cover up what they are doing. Actually, they are civil cases. If you read "Clerk's Praxis", you find that what they call 'criminal' is all civil, they just call it criminal to cover up what their doing. If you don't pay the debt you go to prison, bottom line. I know I've been there. EVERYBODY IS FEEDING OFF OF THE PRISON SYSTEM: ALL OF THE MAJOR CORPORATIONS ARE FEEDING OFF OF THE PRISON SYSTEM. How many of you have heard of REIT = Real Estate Investment Trust or PZN which means Prison Trust? Prisoners are real estate? They own all the real estate because they hold the Bonds on them.

REINSURANCE AGREEMENT FOR A BONDS STATUTE PAYMENT BOND	OMB Control Number: 9000-0045
(See instructions on reverse)	Expiration Date: 7/31/2019

Paperwork Reduction Act Statement - This information collection meets the requirements of 44 USC § 3507, as amended by section 2 of the Paperwork Reduction Act of 1995. You do not need to answer these questions unless we display a valid Office of Management and Budget (OMB) control number. The OMB control number for this collection is 9000-0045. We estimate that it will take 60 minutes to read the instructions, gather the facts, and answer the questions. Send only comments relating to our time estimate, including suggestions for reducing this burden, or any other aspects of this collection of information to: General Services Administration, Regulatory Secretariat Division (MTV1CB), 1800 F Street, NW, Washington, DC 20405.

1. DIRECT WRITING COMPANY*		1A. DATE DIRECT WRITING COMPANY EXECUTES THIS AGREEMENT
		1B. STATE OF INCORPORATION
2. REINSURING COMPANY*		2A. AMOUNT OF THIS REINSURANCE $
		2B. DATE REINSURING COMPANY EXECUTES THIS AGREEMENT
		2C. STATE OF INCORPORATION

3. DESCRIPTION OF CONTRACT		4. DESCRIPTION OF BOND	
3A. AMOUNT OF CONTRACT		4A. PENAL SUM OF BOND	
3B. CONTRACT DATE	3C. CONTRACT NUMBER	4B. DATE OF BOND	4C. BOND NUMBER

You haven't redeemed your Bond, so they didn't close your account. Here's what goes on: A contractor comes in or any corporation could come in and tender a Bid Bond to the US District Court and they buy up these court judgments and anytime you issue a Bid Bond there has to be a reinsure. So they get a Reinsurance Company to come in and act as Surety for the Bid Bond, then they bring in a Performance Bond. All of these Bonds; Bid, Payment & Performance are all Surety Bonds and anytime you issue a Bid Bond it has to have a Surety guaranteeing or reinsuring the Bid Bond via issuing a Performance Bond. Then they get an underwriter and that would be either an Investment Broker or an Investment Banker. They come in and underwrite the Performance Bond which is reinsuring the Bid Bond. What does the underwriter do with the Performance Bond? The underwriter takes the 3 Bonds and pools them and creates what is known as Mortgaged Backed Securities. When you pool these MBS, they are called BONDS and are sold to a company called TBA, which is the Bond Market Association - this is an actual Corporation. These converted Bonds, now MBS' are investment securities and being sold the international level. CCA is one of the tickers on the NY Stock Exchange. Others include; CWX, CWD & CWG. When it goes to Frankfurt = CWG, when it goes to Berlin = CWD and so on. Remember, everything is commercial. 7211 7 CFR says that all crimes are commercial. If you read that carefully it says kidnapping, robbery, extortion, murder, etc. are all commercial crimes. Thus, you are funding the whole enchilada simply because you got into Default Judgment when you went into court and failed to redeem the Bond. This is why people don't win in court; cause they don't redeem the Bond. You are the Principal upon which all money circulates, but you don't want to start arguing with the court about that. They are drafting you for performance. So, anytime the court asks you to do something they are drafting you for performance and if you don't perform, you get into dishonor by non acceptance. They are making a formal presentment under 3-501 of the UCC so they can charge you and they USE the word "charge". They use the same commercial words on your Indictment, Information and Complaint. They use the word "charge", i.e., "the following charges", "...he has two counts of charges", etc. Be as gentle as a dove and wise as a serpent. You can't act like an insurgent or belligerent. If you do, they will treat you like one; they'll beat you up. What you want to do is settle the account...go to full settlement and closure; you're running the account, you're the Fiduciary Trustee over the account – tell them what to do. You're the Principal and owner of the account, tell them what to do – tell them you want full settlement and closure of the account. You have to do this from the get-go. In order to win in court you have to redeem the Bond. Here is where to begin: Start with what we call a conditional acceptance. With the conditional acceptance you can say: "I'm more than happy to give you my name, if you can show that charging papers have been put into the court record. I have not seen any papers that show any charges exist." That's a "Negative Averment". What you are doing is rebutting the presumption that they have charges against you. They work off presumptions. They don't have to have anything. You must rebut their presumptions. I went down there and asked them for the Bid Bond. I said I want the Bid Bond back. I asked for full settlement and closure of the account. It's your money that they create and the same thing is going on in the Banks and with these Bonds - they monetize these Bonds. Then ask for legal counsel. The reason why you have to have an attorney, and I cannot emphasize this too strongly, is because the attorney while in a courtroom is they are working on the public side and you are working on the private side. The court cannot talk to you except through your attorney. You need a mouth piece; a microphone. That is what attorneys are - a mouthpiece. Everyone on the Public side is insolvent and bankrupt. You are not. This is situation is called a Fiction-of-Law. They will not allow you to defeat this "Fiction-Of-Law". Why? In Admiralty Maritime Law everything is colorable. It has the appearance of being real but is not real. They will appoint legal counsel for you. You then instruct the attorney that you are doing a "LETTER OF ROGATORY" or letter of advice. This is also called an "Acceptance for Honor" and you want an accounting of what the total amount of the Bill is post settlement and closure of this account. Then you give your CUSIP and AUTOTIS number and your case number. Here's the wording you use: "I accept your charge(s) for Value and Consideration in return for Post Settlement and Closure of Case # , account# 123-45-6789 [put down your 9 digit social security number] and put down CUSIP# [your ssn] & AUTOTRIS# [your ssn w/o dashes]. Please us my exemption for full settlement and closure of this account as this account is prepaid and exempt from levy. (Date it and endorse it as the Authorized Representative.) (AUTOTRIS means Automated Tracking Identification System. This is the same as your social security number without the dashes. When I said that they didn't even want to talk to me…when you sayCUSIP & AUTOTRIS they know exactly what you're talking about. CUSIP is The COMMITTEE ON UNIFORM SECURITIES IDENTIFICATION PROCESSES. . CUSIP uses your Social Security Number to identify you because the Birth Certificate is a Security. It is an investment security and they have all the original Birth Certificates which are registered at the State level with the Department of Human Recourses and then they go to the Department of Commerce and the Federal level and then to the DTC (Depository Trust Corporation). Judges and lawyers don't understand commercial law. They do not teach commercial law at law school.

They have a special school for them and it's on a "need to know" basis. The law always assumes that you know, since you were doing this since you were born until you reach the age of accountability, which is 18 years of age or what they call adulthood. If your holding yourself out and using commercial paper on a daily basis, that legal definition makes you an expert or you wouldn't be using it, so they presume that when you go into the courtroom you know all this stuff. They have to give you an out. Whenever you create a liability, you always have to create a remedy. They're on the Public side of the accounting ledger. You are on the Private side. You have an account and your account is a "Demand Deposit" account and you are insured by the FDIA and the FDIC. The "Federal Depository

Insurance Act" which insures the FDIC which is the Federal Depository Insurance Corporation under Title 12; they have a $10 Million Dollar Policy on you and YOU'RE WORTH MORE DEAD THAN YOU ARE ALIVE. THEY WILL NEVER TELL YOU THIS STUFF!! NOTE: All tradable Securities must be assigned a CUSIP NUMBER before it can be offered to investors. Birth Certificates and Social Security Applications are converted into Government Securities; assigned a CUSIP NUMBER; grouped into lots and then are marketed as a Mutual Fund Investment.

Upon maturity, the profits are moved into a GOVERNMENT CESTA QUE TRUST and if you are still alive, the certified documents are reinvested. It is the funds contained in this CESTA QUE TRUST that the Judge, Clerk and County Prosecutor are really after or interested in! This Trust actually pays all of your debts but nobody tells you that because the Elite consider those assets to be their property and the Federal Reserve System is responsible for the management of those Investments. Social Security; SSI; SSD; Medicare and Medicaid are all financed by the Trust. The government makes you pay TAXES and a potion of your wages supposedly to pay for these services, which they can borrow at any time for any reason since they cannot access the CESTA QUE TRUST to finance their Wars or to bail out Wall Street and their patron Corporations. The public is encouraged to purchase all kinds of insurance protection when the TRUST actually pays for all physical damages; medical costs; new technology and death benefits. The hype to purchase insurance is a ploy to keep us in poverty and profit off our stupidity because the Vatican owns the controlling interest in all Insurance Companies. You may receive a monthly statement from a Mortgage Company; Loan Company or Utility Company, which usually has already been paid by the TRUST. Almost all of these corporate businesses double dip and hope that you have been conditioned well enough by their Credit Scams, to pay them a second time.

Instead of paying that Statement next time, sign it approved and mail it back to them. If they then contact you about payment, ask them to send you a TRUE BILL instead of a Statement and you will be glad to pay it? A Statement documents what was due and paid, whereas a TRUE BILL represents only what is due. Banks and Utility Companies have direct access into these Cesta Que Trusts and all they needed was your name; social security number and signature

6.   I SELF LAW AM MASTER

The Seven Shades of Wisdom:
1. He who knows not, yet strives to know is a seeker, aid him.
2. He who knows not what he should know is a wanderer, guide him.
3. He who knows not what he should know is asleep, awaken him.
4. He who know not, and fears knowing is a slave, free him.
5. He who knows not, and rejects to know is dead, pass him.
6. He who knows not, but claims to know is an imposter, cast him away.
7. He who knows, and shares what he knows is wise, heed him.

10 RULES OF COMMERCE

1. You can only control that which you create. (Create a child)

2. You can not control that which you did not create. (State has no control over child)
3. All of commerce is based on Title. (Birth certificate, MSO, copyright)
4. The only true Title to anything is the MSO. (Geneses 1 verse 1)
5. When you register anything anywhere you give up Title. (Car, Child, vote)
6. There is no Money/ (there is no Spoon). (Only credit in circulation Public, and private)
7. There is no involuntary Servitude.
8. First in line is first in time. (Recorded into public record at county)
9. Do not interfere with commerce.
10. Allow nothing to come between you and your Creator.
(Examples) A. My Divorce B. Biker Billy Lane C speeding with MCO Applying these rules can help us to understand and even master commerce.

Commerce as we know it began in Babylon; we see how commerce began with Daniel's interpretation of king Nebuchadnezzar's dream.

The dream is about a body and the body is clad in various metals from head to toe, each metal represents a civilization from Babylon to present, the important part of the dream is the body, or corp.C.

The body has to do with all of commerce as we know it, Corporations are dead bodies. Commercial rules are in Probate because dead bodies, dead corporations are all in probate. (All commercial contracts are in Probate (except) a will is the only commercial agreement that survives death) Commerce deals with the Unorganic and deals with nothing from the Earth

Ecclesiastical Law is the body of law derived from canon and civil law and administered by the ecclesiastical courts. Ecclesiastical law governs the doctrine of a specific church, usually, Anglican canon law. Ecclesiastical law is also termed as jus ecclesisasticum or law spiritual.

Ecclesiastical courts were established to hear matters concerning the religion. The jurisdiction exercised by ecclesiastical courts played a major role in the development of the English legal system. Their duties and work were not limited to the controlling of clergies and doctrines of the Church. Before the Reformation, the ecclesiastical courts had significant jurisdiction. In matters relating to matrimonial causes and testate and intestate succession, the law remained significant and relevant until the mid of the nineteenth century.

Since ecclesiastical courts were not established in the United States, the code of laws enforced in such courts could not be considered part of the common law that existed in the colonies. It has also been stated that the canon and civil laws administered by the ecclesiastical courts of England should be grouped along with the unwritten laws of England which were adopted and used in certain jurisdiction. Therefore, it is argued that such laws should be employed where the rule of the ecclesiastical courts is deemed to be better law than the rule announced by a common law court.

PART TWO THE PUBLIC SIDE

TO BE CONTINUED....

$1 MILLION WORTH OF GAME

$1 MILLION WORTH OF GAME

MALIK KILAM

1. The Sole Proprietor (The Sole Trader)
2. Building The Sole Trader's Credit
3. Building Your Brand
4. Building The Business Credit & Fundability
5. Kilam's Top 10 100k+ Online Business Revenue
6. Importance of Holding Companies
7. Asset Protection

ADDEDD BONUS HOW WHAT WOULD MALIK KILAM SAY TO A BANK TO OBTAIN BUSINESS FUNDING AQUISITION!

THE PUBLIC SIDE WILL ALSO GRANT YOU ACCESS TO YOU FREE BUSINESS TRUST MANAUAL

DON KILAM TRUST CO.
and
MALIK KILAM
PRESENTS:

Black Americans have an annual spending power of $1.2 trillion, their households only held a median of $11,000 of wealth in 2013, according to federal data. What's even more disturbing is that by 2053, the median wealth for black families will fall to zero if the gap continues to widen at its current pace. Median wealth for white Americans is 12 times higher than that of black Americans at around $140,000, and the inequality in wealth continues to grow and widen with each generation. Just in the past 30 years, which is around the median age of a millennial, white families' wealth has grown three times that of a black family, the Institute for Policy Studies shared.

Generational wealth, financial assets that are passed on and built upon with each generation within a family, is particularly important to future financial security. It's the foundation for opportunities and access to better education, health, and jobs.

The racial wealth gap "starts with our nation's history of institutionalized racism, discrimination, bias, and restriction from information and opportunity," says Rodney Sampson, cofounder of Opportunity Hub (OHUB), the largest black-owned multi-campus entrepreneurship center and technology hub in the U.S. "Although these constructs remain today," he says, "black Americans through exposure, knowledge and access to work, entrepreneurship, and investment opportunities in the innovation economy have the greatest opportunity to create new multi-generational wealth with no reliance on pre-existing multi-generational wealth."

$1 MILLION
WORTH OF GAME

MALIK KILAM

1.The Sole Proprietor (The Sole Trader)
2.Building The Sole Trader's Credit
3.Building Your Brand
4.Building The Business Credit & Fundability
5.Importance of Holding Companies
6.Estate Planning & Asset Protection
7.Kilam's Top 10 100k+ Online Business Revenue

The Sole Proprietor (The Sole Trader)

In a debate between Hillary Clinton and Donald Trump during the last election, Donald Trump made a statement to rebuttal Hillary's attack on him for not paying as much taxes as the average American Citizen.

Now President Trump, replied by saying "I don't **pay as much taxes because I *kno*w about the loopholes and laws that allow me to NOT pay personal income taxes."**
By understanding the foundations of the SSN, IRS, EIN, and LLC's Corporations, and pass through trust. Donald J. Trump uses to earn money, get business loans, and NOT pay a lot, or any income taxes too.

When I was taught about these loopholes, policies, and laws by a billionaire mentor back in the 2014, he told me **to always look and learn about the foundations, seeds, and roots of things first**. Then everything else would make more sense. After over 5 years of thinking and acting this way, I can confirm that he was 100% right!

The foundations of the systems in place that governs and influences our financial lifestyles can be found within the Federal Reserve Banking Systems, The Department of Revenue, IRS, and the Social Security Administration. Sure, there are a few more agencies and organizations that affect our daily lives, such as the Credit Reporting Agencies and Banks. However, in order to successfully build your Personal Credit and Business Credit in ways that lead to wealth creation, you simply need to **internalize the foundational objectives of the departments that created the SSN & EIN**
Department of Revenue found systems that enables them to look through millions of records of *companies,* and find them easily through the utilization of *identification numbers* just like Social Security Numbers. The EIN
and SSN were actually established alongside each other with the same perspectives. Most Citizens of America never take these perspectives in to account. The government seeks to earn money from taxes and other things from both Citizens and Businesses. Therefore, they could care less which one you choose to identify yourself by, and, or use to build credit. In fact, after interviewing several government agency employees, most of them have admitted that **our government would prefer Citizens find ways to become businesses.** Why? Well once again, the truth is hidden in plain

sight. Most Americans do NOT know that as basic Citizens, we are not required to pay income taxes. Yet, from the mass confusion, this voluntary act almost seems mandatory just like the use of the Social Security Number.

For these reasons, the government has created what recent conspiracy theorist refer to as "The Strawman," to do business with each American. Have ever noticed on your Driver's License, SSN Card, and other government documents, your name is in all CAPITAL LETTERS? This is there way of calling you a "Business/Corporation" instead of an average citizen.

According to Business Dictionary.com, one of the definitions of a <u>Strawman</u> is "A Third-**party set up to serve as a cover (to conceal the identity of the actual party)** in accomplishing **a shady deal or something not legally permitted.**

Unfortunately, this is exactly what these government agencies have done to the majority of American Citizens.

The government uses to identify you. Unfortunately, after accepting these names as our identifiers, most of us have been conditioned to think that our "LEGAL NAMES" are actually who we are. In reality, our legal names are not who we are, because each of us is a man or a woman with a body made of flesh and blood.

Names are not real, living, breathing *people,* but instead are symbols of things (non-beings). In legal terms, names are artificial persons which are corporations. In other words, your legal name represents the corporate name that is used by the government to identify yo*u.*

WHY DOES THE GOVERNMENT DO THIS?

To start, we must understand and remember that the United States of America is not truly a nation alone, but a **"Corporation" too. That's right, the so called country that you know as The United States of America is NOT a general country. It is a Corporat**ion! That's right, just like you are learning, for the sake of "identification" and "use," the powers that control the USA have made many believe they were not a Corporation and, or controlled by Corporations.

Let's re-examine Corporations and why the elite hides behind it:

Dictionary

corporation

cor po ra tion / korpe
raSH(e)n/

noun

a company or group of people authorized to act as a single entity
(legally a person) and recognized as such in law Synonyms company
furm business concem operation house organization Agency trust
partnership:
More
• a group of people elected to govern a city,
town, or borough
noun: municipal corporation; plural noun
municipal Corporations - dated' humorous
a
paunch.

Translations, word origin, and more
definitions

Feedback

Corporation | Definition of Corporation by Merriam-Webster
https://www.merriam-webster.com/dictionary/corporation » Define
corporation a group of merchants or traders united in a trade guild: the
municipal authorities of a town or city — corporation in a sentence.

Legally a PERSON, and recognized as such in law?!?

Does this definition sound a little like how you have already been treated as a Citizen of
the United States? The truth is this is exactly how they see you. If you follow me on
youtube Don Kilam or Malik Kilam Legacy, I talk a lot about how the United States has
tricked most of its Citizens into middle class living without a spiritual, mental, physical
and financial way out. For now, I am committed to use words to set you free via
establishing your own business identity.

Like your "Legal Name," the government is also not real because it is a Corporation. According to Black's Law dictionary 6th edition, a **Corporation is an artificial person**" or "legal entity" **created by or under the authority of the laws of a state.** Yet, it can and does go into business and contractual agreements with YOU. Therefore, in order to even the playing ground, you simply need to do the same thing. Become a Corporation.

Because the government is a Corporation (artificial person), it is a fictitious entity that should not have any *natural* rights and powers. Yet, this is Not the case.

For those of you who still do not understand, let me give you some examples:

When you hear the name "**MICHAEL JORDAN**" or even "**DONALD J.**

TRUMP" you don't know if they are talking about **the Corporation or the Human Being.** More than likely, if it has anything to do with their banking, credit, or even advertisements, they are talking about their Corporation.

Now, if you think about what I stated about the government treating us like Corporations to begin with, and how they create a Strawman for us, it is easy to see how we take it back. If we were to go to court behind some legal document such as a Lease, Traffic Ticket, or any other Strawman activity, we can easily tell the court "**You have no jurisdiction over me!**" Why? The answer is mainly because most Corporations must be tried in Civil Court, and even if you are being tried as a member of your Corporation, it must be distinguished and determined as such.

I even know people who sign traffic tickets and other legal documents as their Corporations to avoid going to court. *Shhh...* if done correctly,

most Police Officers DO NOT know the difference. Under law, when a judge discovers this, tickets and other charges are dismissed because of lack of jurisdiction.

Another great example of this, is a Physician that works for a Hospital. Being that most Hospitals and Physician Groups are Non-Profit Organizations, and understand the difficulties Physicians can have in filing taxes, they have no problem paying their employees via 1099 and their EIN. Many other Employers also have no problem paying their Employees via 1099 and their EIN, such as Real Estate Brokers, Construction Companies, Contractors, and more.

Nevertheless, **99% of all wealthy individuals I know use their "Personal Names" as Corporations**. If you know the differences in benefits of a Corporation as opposed to a

Sole Proprietor, you should already know why. However, let's look at some of the financial reasons:

As a Corporation instead of a Sole Proprietor, you can:

> 1. Take control of your Legal Name/Strawman 2. Keep yourself separate from lawsuits and protect your assets 3. Build Credit Faster 4. Save on Taxes 5. Function as a Real Separate Legal Entity 6. Get Employers to PAY you via 1099

Repairing Bad Backgrounds Initially, we weren't going to include this topic within this course because of a question of ethics. However, as we read into the laws of how "NAMES" are being used against human beings, we decided to provide information and leave it up to our students to do what they will, just like everything else we discuss in our courses.

To help you understand how a lot of our students are going on to succeed with EINs and completely avoiding, and, or repairing bad personal backgrounds.,

To help you internalize this even more, let's take a look at the laws of **"CHANGING YOUR NAME."**

In most states you can legally change your name simply through "usage.*" Yes*, right now, you can choose a new name and just start using it. This act alone is considered a legal name change. However, like our student above, to avoid issues with the government and businesses you decide to do business with, it's best to make it official by filing it with the courts. Remember, every state is different when it comes to their name change procedures, be sure to check with your local court clerk to learn about your state's requirements.

Additionally, there are certain forms of identification, such as social security cards and passports which will require "legal name change documents." Therefore, instead of arguing, why not just file it with the courts and receive them?"

Just like everything else, there are certain steps required in order to accomplish what you need and desire from deciding to change your name.

WHY THE GOVERNMENT LIKES CORPORATIONS?

Just as **the Law of Sowing and Reaping** has been proven in every aspect of life, **the Law of Association** has too. If you think and act like the wealthy, you will become wealthy. Therefore, for the sake of giving you proper perspective of the powers of the EIN, I am about to share with you the foundations of MONEY earning in America that 99% of Americans do Not have.

I can't stress enough how important it is to always have the right perspectives about the main things that effect your life. **Perspectives determine how we act at all times.** Therefore, having proper perspectives can make your life instantly better, just like bad perspectives can drive you down and keep you there.

One perspective of the US Government is that i**t would prefer to do business with real and registered Corporations as opposed to Fictitious and Strawmen Citizens (You and** I). Why?

The answer should be obviously because it needs and wants money to prosper and grow. While this was an honest reason, common sense would have told the founders that this *money would have had to come from American Businesses going outside of America to earn money and bring it back home*. This didn't happen! Therefore, the next idea was to magically create the illusion of wealth. By doing this, America could turn into the biggest Attraction and Theme Park in the world for others to move to, do business with, and ultimately become the wealthiest right? Wrong! Although other nations and its citizens did become attracted to America enough to visit, relocate to it, and do business with it, it just wasn't enough. Therefore, the next step was to try and TAX its Businesses/Corporations again. Th**is was the true motive of turning Corporations into Fictitious Citizens and Citizens into Fictitious Corporations.**

With this perspective becoming a stronghold over time, I am 100% convinced that the foundations of the United States of America is designed in ways that automatically prevents its Citizens from ever becoming wealthy. Regardless of what you do as a Citizen, the odds are stacked against you becoming wealthy. Why? Again, America has to earn and receive money from somewhere in order to stand as a prosperous nation. Therefore, it believes granting rights and advantages to Corporations more than it Citizens will get it there. As a backup plan it also believes that treating Citizens as Corporations without granting them the rights given to Corporations will also help to build its monetary value. This is why, as Citizens, we are considered to be in Debt and why we all feel an inner conflict we can't explain!

I've seen doctors, professional athletes, musicians and others who receive millions of dollars live just above, or right at the middle class level. On the other hand, I have seen the average citizen with a middle class income become wealthy by following the perspectives of the EIN I am sharing with you.

Although the government looks at you and I as Corporations when it comes to taking our money, it treats us as Citizens when it comes to everything else. Let's think about this a little more...

Corporation - It Consumes ONLY for the purpose of *Earning* Money

Citizen - It Consumes ONLY for the purpose of S*pending* Money

Those who are privy to consistently think this way, understand that everything from Clothing, Housing, Gas, Mileage, Food, and more, will be conside**red consumption for the purposes of Earning Money under their Corporations**, as opposed to living as **a Citizen that consumes for the purpose o*f Interest* and *Spending* Money**. Please **INVEST** your attention in the word "**Interest**" for a moment.

Would you be INETERESTED in knowing the **ONLY way to truly earn money in America?**

If so, the answer is **INTEREST (**Energy). Yes, it's that simple!

INTEREST is the ONLY way to gain money in America

Most people would argue that Profits from Sales is a way of gaining money in America. Yet, if you follow the process of money after most

sales are made, you will discover "Interest," hiding in the midst and at the end of all monies earned from Sales.

INTEREST is what the government and most major corporations live on. Yet, we have been taught as Citizens to be and stay on the other end of this energy.

CORPORATIONS - It GAINS from Interest

CITIZENS - It SPENDs for Interest

Energy + TIME makes INTEREST WORK! Interest makes people work!

A good way to internalize this is to think about Slavery. *W*hen wealthy Americans thought about generating millions of dollars back then, the main way was via the Slave

Trade. The more slaves you had working for you for FREE, the more value you held in terms of Interest. Unfortunately, this is exactly how our so-called government thinks today. From Taxes to Fractional Banking, the US Government/Corporation earns and receives Interest from each and

every one of us like Slaves.

We work hard to earn a little money, and then turn around and borrow money for houses, cars, credit cards, and education to pay them INTEREST. Why? We are all INTERESTED in these things.

To make it even worse, we pay even more Interest by way of paying taxes on our incomes first, and then for food, clothes, housing, and more. Now ask yourself **"Regardless of how much money you earn,**

can you ever get and stay rich in America living this way?" Of course not!

Now on the other hand, ask yourself **"If you become a Corporation like the United States and others, can you become wealthy in America?"** Of course you can!

Other than establishing your new EIN for the sake of Credit and Identification, it is your pathway to Wealth creation. It's the reason why I named this course and eBook "The EIN **Secret to Wealth."**

By establishing and using your EIN, you can not only begin earning money from developing Interest Gaining instruments, you can also begin saving money on things such as taxes, clothing, travel, food, entertainment, and more. Now that you have some idea of what you can do with a new EIN, let's get it started...

HOW TO ESTABLISH YOUR *EIN* Successfully?

So now you know what a EIN is and why the wealthy use it 100% legally to establish credit, banking, asset protection, and PERSONAL IDENTITY!

Building The Sole Trader's Credit

We have already discussed how to dispute your personal credit and you do this for hard inquiries and past accounts as well! Make Sure you do this before building your personal credit.

Tradelines and primary accounts

First, what is a tradeline? A tradeline is the industry term for any credit account that appears on your credit report. We evaluate your credit reports to see if tradelines will help; if so, we get your data, submit it to the lender (e.g. Chase, Bank of America, Discover, etc) and the lender reports the data to the credit bureaus. When this data posts, your score will experience a boost.

What makes tradelines so effective? Glad you asked.

First, have a look at how the 3 credit bureaus evaluate your score.

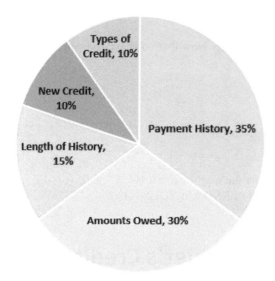

Tradelines provide positive data on three evaluation factors:

Payment History

Amount owed

Length of History

These factors comprise as much as 60% of your credit score. When we post an AU, you are benefiting from the age of the tradeline, the availability of the limit (always utilized under 10%), and the perfect payment history.

Looking at the credit scale is like looking at the grading scale back in school.

FICO Score ranges from 350 – 850, where 350 being the lowest credit score and 850 being the highest:

- 350-579 – Poor – F Grade
- 580-619 – Below Average – D Grade
- 620-659 – Average -C Grade
- 660-719 – Good – B Grade
- 720-850 – Excellent – A Grade

Tradelines can help move you an entire grade, which could be the difference in getting an approval, or that next rate tier, saving you thousands over the course of the loan.

Primaries are better for your account

We like primaries over tradelines

Tradelines are just lines of credit such as Macys or a JC Pennys you may also be added as an authorized users. So you may or may not be able to utilize someone elses credit to help boost your credit.

Unsecured credit that are guaranteed

$99 to join $5,000 worth of credit that never falls off

https://www.agjewelrydesign.com/

Attractive Gems Jewelers $10,000.00 revolving credit line with 24-month 0% financing gives you an opportunity to obtain a Credit card even if you have bad credit, we believe in giving everyone with or without credit a chance! and hope to gain happy customers for years to come.

YOUR APPROVAL IS GUARANTEED as long as you meet the below criteria:

Attractive Gems Jewelers $10,000 revolving credit line has a onetime membership fee of $149.99 and an annual maintenance fee of $99.99

https://getthatjewelry.com/

between the $7,500 and the $10,000.

https://shopsimplio.com/

$8,500 of Unsecured Revolving Credit within 48-72hrs!

MAGNUM® 4500

$**49.50** /mo

- $4,500 Installment Account Reported

PRIMARY TRADELINES

As negative items are starting to be removed from your credit report. We recommend you start adding new primary tradelines. These new active accounts will help boost your credit score. Please choose 3 – 4 from the following list below if you don't have any primary tradeline, 2 – 3 if you have at-least one primary tradeline.

MJC□ Offers up to $5,000 unsecured revolving credit an reports to all 3 bureaus monthly□ Click Here

CreditBuilderCard

Credit Builder Card – Get a secured credit card with as little as a $200 – $1000 Deposit. No credit score needed for approval. Reports to all 3 credit bureaus. Click Here

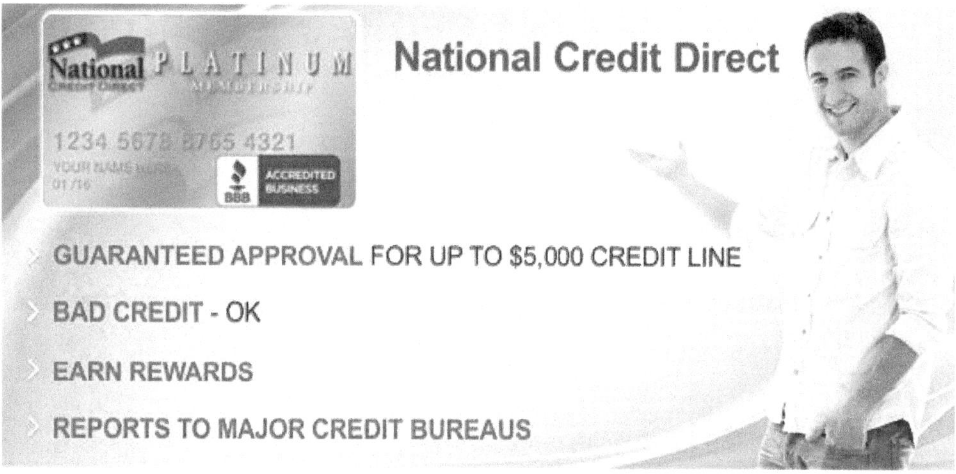

National Credit Direct – Guaranteed Approval Up to $5000 in unsecured revolving credit. No Hidden Fees or interest charges, Member Benefits, and Unlimited Customer Support. Reward Points Program, which is similar to major credit cards or airline miles. Reports to all 3 credit bureaus. Click Here

WHAT TO EXPECT FROM YOUR CREDIT STRONG ACCOUNT?

 NO CREDIT SCORE REQUIRED

 NO HARD CREDIT INQUIRY

 NO UPFRONT SECURITY DEPOSIT

Build credit history while saving. Austin Capital Bank gives you an installment loan. You do not receive the funds on day one, they are instantly deposited into the savings account. A lock is placed on the funds in the savings account to secure the loan. Each month you make a single, fixed monthly payment of principal and interest on the loan. The principal portion of your loan payment is credited towards the lock on your savings account and the interest portion of your payment is how we cover the costs of providing the service to you. During the term of your account we report your loan payment history to all three major credit bureaus and you earn interest on your savings account balance.

When the loan is paid in-full, the lock is removed from the savings account and the funds become available to you. Click Here

Membership program for only from $99.99 to start and from $29.99 monthly & we report your new $7,500.00 or $10,000.00 revolving account to all three credit bureaus. Click Here

Open a Credit Builder Account, pay monthly and on time to build positive payment history. Self will help establish the regular payment history that is key to building credit.

No Upfront Deposit. Get Approved in Minutes. Withdraw Savings at End. Reports to all three credit bureaus. Click Here

NCD – offer you up to $5,000 unsecured revolving credit line so you can finance the latest technology, electronics, household items and more. Reports to Equifax and Transunion. Click Here

Rent Reporters – RentReporters is here to help the nearly 100 million renters improve their credit by reporting their on-time rent payment history to the credit bureaus. Rent Payments can Boost your Credit Score with the average Credit Score Increase is 40 Points. Reports to Equifax and Transunion.⬜Click Here

Hutton Chase – Guaranteed Approval! $1,500 Credit Line. Purchase online (Electronics, Apparel & Accessories, Cookware, Jewelries and etc.) Will help you Boost your Score. Reports to Equifax and Experian. Click Here

Ox Publishing – Love Reading Books? Boost your Score While reading your favorite books! Purchase online E-Book source. Reports to Equifax and Experian. Click Here

https://www.callcreditpro.com/

https://www.loqbox.com/en_us/how-it-works

https://tomocredit.com/?referral=BnsgUq

X1 Credit Card A Soft Inquiry Credit Check Card? We will find out. Please Waitlist Now: https://x1creditcard.com/r/POVqlej

Tomo Fintech Debit/Credit Card. $100 - $10,000 Credit limit - No Hard Inquiry - Waitlist: https://tomocredit.com/?referral=BnsgUq

Salt Lending For Crypto Currency Investors. Use your crypto to get lines of credit: https://saltlending.com/

After you build your credit you can buy and sell tradelines as authorized user get paid

Building Your Brand

There are a lot of misconceptions about what it takes to run a successful online business. I find that even experienced business owners often underestimate the time, energy and skill it takes to really succeed online.

This post will look at 21 "secret" facts that set successful online businesses apart from the rest. If you want to succeed at building your online empire. Take note.

1. They grow fast.

While it's rare that an online business becomes an overnight success, it's just as rare for it to take more than a couple of years. This is particularly true in very competitive niches. If you're a year or two in and haven't grown at all, it's probably time to reevaluate your business model.

2. They leverage amazing tools to save time and money.

I challenge you to find a single, successful online business that doesn't rely on *at least* 5-10 amazing tools to run their business. In fact, I'd argue that tools are an absolute necessity for *every* online business. From <u>social media management tools</u> to <u>online invoicing tools</u>, to <u>team communication tools</u>, these are key to saving you time and money and optimizing your productivity.

3. Part of being successful is knowing when to give up.

I could list a bunch of "never give up" quotes here, but that would just contradict my point. Successful online business owners know that sometimes you absolutely MUST cut your losses and generally there will be something or someone you have to give up on. It may be a strategy, a person or even on an entire business venture.

A good rule of thumb: if trusted advisors or colleagues are telling you it's time to give up on something, do yourself a favor -- listen and consider what is being said. You can't keep track of everything.

Advertising tycoon David Ogilvy famously said, "Hire people better than you are, then leave them to get on with it." The same goes for outsourcing. If you want to stay competitive, outsource everything that a) doesn't come naturally to you, and b) that you don't enjoy doing. This will free you up to focus on what you love, which is key to sustainable growth.

5. Social media is their not-so-secret weapon.

You cannot run a successful online business without using social media. Just over two years ago, Shareholic revealed that <u>almost a third of all referral traffic was from social media</u>. I suspect this number is significantly higher today. If you're not using social media to reach new customers and to connect with current ones, you don't stand a chance.

6. They know that passive income is never totally passive.

Many people have this idea that running an online business allows you to work minimal hours while sipping a margarita on the beach. And while it *does* give you far more flexibility than a traditional job, "passive income" is a bit of a misnomer. Even if your business is highly automated and can run largely without your hands-on involvement, most online businesses will still require you to oversee and manage the big picture tasks (which, admittedly, you can often do while laying on the beach).

7. They focus on the big picture.

Running an online business isn't for everyone. If you tend to spend more time on details than you do on setting goals, making plans, looking for trends, etc., running an online business may not be the path for you.

8. They know the value they provide - and charge accordingly.

You'll never compete long term by undervaluing your products or services. While it may be tempting initially to undercut the competition in order to make a name for yourself, it's almost always better to set prices that are sustainable for your business for the foreseeable future.

9. They grow their list from day one.

Email marketing is an important strategy for all businesses. But for online businesses, it's absolutely vital. Research is clear that email marketing results in increased click-through rates, engagement, and sales. In fact, some research suggests email delivers a higher ROI than any other marketing channel. Focus on building your list from day one to see these benefits for your own business.

10. They solve a real problem.

As with any type of business, finding a real need in your niche is key. What problem or issue can you help solve? Does your product or service truly solve that problem? If not, what can you do to make that happen?

11. They differentiate themselves.

Just how big is the global e-commerce market? Some estimate that it's a trillion dollar market spread among 12 million online stores. Successful online business owners know the importance of differentiating themselves so they can actually claim their piece of the pie.

12. They understand the value of amazing content.

Content marketing isn't optional anymore, especially for online businesses. If you're not producing a steady stream of relevant, valuable content, you don't have a chance of being successful. Not sure where to start? Check out my comprehensive content marketing guide.

13. They go all in.

Some people think they can build an online empire in their spare time. They put most of their time and effort into their 9-5 job, then fiddle with their business when they feel like it. Successful online businesses are rarely built this way. If you treat it like a hobby, it will stay a hobby. Give your online business the attention it deserves and treats it like the real business it is.

14. They listen to their customers.

Don't underestimate the value your customers bring to the process of growing and developing your online business. Nella Chunky, the founder of hugely successful clothing company Fresh-Tops, believes customer suggestions were key to her startup's success: "We relied on email requests and suggestions from our social media fans when deciding how to move forward and what items to add to our line, and it worked really well."

15. They pursue their passion.

Running an online business can be tough, which is why it's so important you're passionate about what you're doing. Ask yourself: Can I see myself still be in this business in 5-10 years? If not, it's probably better to shift directions and choose something you really care about.

16. They invest heavily in SEO.

According to <u>research</u> from Ascend2, *82%* of marketers believe the effectiveness of SEO is on the rise. Getting high rankings in the search engines is imperative for an online business, as this will likely be one of your largest sources of traffic. Need some help with optimizing your site?

17. They take action even before everything's perfect.

Ryan French, Creator of GameKlip has <u>great advice</u> for new business owners: don't wait until everything's perfect to get moving. He writes, "Don't feel like you need to know everything, or that everything has to be perfect before you start. I knew nothing about running a business, had no idea how to have something manufactured, and had no idea how to ship a package overseas. I've now shipped thousands of units to over 80 countries worldwide. It won't be easy, there'll be many points where you feel like giving up, but it's worth it."

18. They stop looking for the golden goose.

There is no magic bullet when it comes to building a successful online business. Yet many business owners waste a ton of time looking for that one tactic or strategy that will catapult them to success. The truth is, if there *were* a golden goose, it would be persistence and hard work. Forget trying to find that one magical thing, put your head down, and do the hard work of running your business.

19. They have an actual plan (a written one).

Another common misconception about online businesses: people just kind of find your website, buy your stuff, and you start making tons of money. This isn't true for brick and mortar businesses, and it definitely isn't true for online ones! Successful online businesses benefit greatly from a solid business plan, as well as a documented marketing strategy.

20. They don't let failure beat them up.

As with any business, failure is just part of the landscape. It's *what you do when you fail* that counts. SEO strategy not driving traffic? Choose different keywords. Content marketing failing? Focus on more in-depth content. Social media posts not getting engagement? Study your competitors to see what you can emulate (or do better).

21. They're dominating their niche.

If you take one thing from this post, let it be this: don't bang your head against the wall trying to compete with the big guys. Instead, niche down and focus on a subset of your industry - and do whatever you can to dominate in that area. For instance, one of my first niches was Christmas tree storage.

Instead of targeting the entire holiday decor industry, we focused exclusively on building our reputation as offering the best storage at the lowest prices. We quickly built a 7-figure business using this strategy - something we could have never done if we had gone after the big guys!

These days, your online platform is crucial. Consumers trust brands more readily if they have an online presence, and per Vox, top tier influencers with substantial followings are now raking in a whopping $100,000 per sponsored post. Online platforms are as lucrative as they are important for customer engagement. And, believe it or not, they're continuing to grow.

According to Brand Watch, even though there are 3.5 billion social media users in the world, another newcomer creates an account every 6.4 seconds. With almost everyone online -- and with that number growing daily -- the sheer potential of your online platform for building a business or sharing your message should not be taken lightly.

But, there is one potential disadvantage of having everyone online: the competition is fierce. Everyone is vying for the engagement of an audience. So, how do you start an online business and scale your online platform so your content can perform and convert followers to customers? Here are some ideas:

Keep churning out content.

It can be discouraging when you keep posting content and nothing seems to take off. The secret is to just keep going! Case Kenny is the host of the "New Mindset, Who Dis?" podcast. It found success initially, but several months in, he wasn't hitting the download numbers he was looking for, which was frustrating for him. Now, his podcast has hit close to 2 million downloads.

"I considered calling it quits. Fortunately, I didn't, I put my head down and kept publishing, fine-tuning my voice and message and in October 2018, the podcast blew up. It ranked #26 in the world on the charts and #8 in the world as a self-help podcast," Kenny shared. It's similar to what Gary Vaynerchuk says frequently: "You're only one piece of content away from what you want to happen happening." The more content you put out, the more likely you are to create that one thing that goes viral and scales your platform.

Be willing to invest in the build process when you start an online business.

Peter Pru, the founder of ECommerce Empire Builders, learned all about scaling an online ecommerce platform through dropshipping. "It takes money to make money," Pru said. He encourages anyone who needs to work part-time or even a full-time job to fund their business to do it. "Almost every startup needs money to begin, so you have to be willing to do what it takes to earn that money so you can invest in yourself and your business."

Investing in a publicist who can get you media exposure or a social media strategist who can help grow your platform is a great use of funds to get you started. Whatever you do, do *not* invest in buying fake followers. These will hurt your engagement rate and can be very obvious to new potential followers who can come across your page.

Learn how to track conversions and data.

Whichever online platforms you use, it's crucial to take stock on what's working and what isn't. Nowadays, there are a number of tracking or analysis tools to help you determine which type of content yields the highest engagement rate. The first element to look at is which social media pages drive the most traffic to your website. Hootsuite recommends using Google Analytics to evaluate this. For example, if your Instagram is sending 18 followers a day to your page but your YouTube is only sending three, you know to focus more effort on Instagram.

Instagram has a built-in feature for business pages that can tell you how well your post does. When you click "View Insights" on a certain post, you'll be able to see the number of impressions and compare it to the number of engagements (likes and comments). Perhaps photos with your face perform better than quote pictures you make in Canva, or maybe videos bring in more comments than just photographs. The next step is to use the data you derive from these analytics to pivot in your strategies moving forward, so you're always doing what drives the most engagement.

Building The Business Credit & Fundability

Unlimited Business Credit Loans

Introduction

There are videos that go with this written package. These videos deeply explain each step of the process. Please watch each companion video as you follow this process.

Also, please read each step fully **twice** before starting, **twice**. If you start this process a while after you read it, please **re-read** it so you are fully ready to take the steps you need to access corporate credit.

Before we get deeply into the process, let's take a minute to talk about what the most effective use of this tool is.

First, and most obviously, an existing ongoing business can access credit to enhance its operations. Not many businesses know how to gain access to credit with no personal liability and use their personal credit to try to get credit for their business. The process of corporate credit eliminates that need.

Second, the most effective use of this tool is for new or nearly new businesses, which have no access to credit until they learn how to take the steps in this package to get credit for your new business with no personal liability. Few people know how to gain access to corporate credit with no personal liability so they are again usually using their personal credit to start operations.

Tips Before We Begin

- Do this process for your business and grow it over time.

- Don't be in a hurry. Just get it right. It takes a bit of time for things to report but if you do the steps correctly you can cut many years off the time it would usually take to create business credit with no personal liability with useful accounts.

- Do this process only for a real business, not a fake one. Why? Many people think when they see this corporate credit package that you can make as many fake businesses as you want and take as much money as you want. While this has some elements of truth in the statement, it is too much work to build business credit for a fake business. It makes sense to start a real business that will be ongoing with its own website, email, clientele, etc. because you might as well grow a revenue stream that will not end if the business were to go bankrupt. How? Watch the companion video that goes over this point in detail.

- If your personal credit is a mess, then corporate credit is a way to operate a trust with great credit and have no personal liability. A trust protects you, your family and your assets. Get the common law irrevocable ecclesiastical trust as it is non-taxable. You can get this from MalikKilam.Com. or Donkilam.com No one should operate a person and everyone should operate a trust. A person is what you operate from the social security number you were given upon birth. The corporate credit methods allow you to operate a trust with better and more credit than you can get personally.

About The Process

Itself

A quick overview of the corporate credit building process is that one must correctly build the corporation to make it possible to build corporate credit.

If the corporation is not initially built correctly, it will never be able to access corporate credit with no personal liability.

It's like building a house, it must have a good foundation.

Once the corporation is built correctly, then the credit of the corporation needs to be built step by step, exactly correctly to make this corporation look credit worthy to all lenders on their software they access to determine lendability.

Knowing what lenders look at to determine lendability is what this portion of the corporate credit building information teaches you.

Terms to Know

When we talk about **corporate credit** we mean credit for any **business** type that is not a person.

A **person** can be called **personal** too. This information does not concern building credit for a person or personal credit. In fact, corporate credit can be built no matter how bad your personal credit is. However, it is far better to have great personal credit.

Please Notice

If you do not have excellent or good personal credit and want to achieve that goal, We assist with that process and other methods such as building credit for the Trust but as I said, you do not have to have good personal credit for the corporate credit process, it is just easier if you do have good personal credit.

Creating a corporation that is lendable is what this process explains. The first step is creating a corporation worthy of credit. This means you have to build that corporation with the exact same attributes a lender needs to build credit. First step is the creation of the corporation with these lendable attributes. Let's go through the checklist of the steps you will take to create what a lender needs to see.

- URL

- Corporation Type

- Register with the Secretary of State

- Name

- Address

- EIN

- Phone Number

- 411 Listing

- Email

- Bank Account

- Dun & Bradstreet Number

- Google Maps

Let's go over and explain the WHY and HOW of each step:

WEBSITE URL

• Get a URL that matches the name of your business. If you can't get an inexpensive readily available URL for your website then move on to another name of the business. (.org, .net, .com or any TLD works) You can look up to see if a URL is available on many services. For example: www.godaddy.com or Shopify

• This website will become the URL address for you corporation's website.

• Get a way to get receive money (PayPal, Stripe, Authorize.net, Skrill, Shopify has its own and many others also utilizing Quicken.Com is great etc.)

• Start a brand new account (I suggest Stripe) as your primary payment gateway.

• Start a brand new account (I suggest PayPal) as your backup payment gateway.

• Whatever payment gateway you choose, check to make sure that the payment gateway will work with your website's CMS (Content Management System).

CORPORATION TYPE

• This item is important to get correct, as not all corporation types are useful in this process. One entity type to steer clear of is an LLC. An LLC is a flow through entity meaning the taxes flow through to your person. Having NO personal liability or connection is important, so the LLC is out. That leaves 3 types of corporations that you can build credit with.

• The 3 types of corporations you CAN build corporate credit with are a non-profit, trust or C corporation. A non-profit is not optimal and should only be used in rare circumstances for specific reasons. That really leaves the C corporation and the trust.

• Let's go over the **C Corporations** first. Often referred to as a C corp. A C corp. is created at the Secretary of State in the state you want to operate this C corporation. C corporation is also called a for profit corporation. *This is a taxable entity.* You can use this... or you can use a...

• Bulletproof Trust. The trust is the other option for a corporation type. But don't use any type of trust. Only use the IrrevcableTrust will truly work for this. Also known as a Common Law Irrevocable Ecclesiastical Trust. *This is not a taxable entity.*

REGISTER WITH SECRETARY OF STATE

• The only extra step that is definitely needed so your credit accounts propagate properly to the business credit bureaus is to register the trust your state's secretary of state. In Florida it costs $350 to register a common law trust with the Secretary of State. You will need to check the cost for your state.

• A for-profit C corporation should automatically be shown on the Secretary of State website but check to make sure.

NAME

• The name of the corporation or trust should match the name of the business, website, etc.

• A trust may also have another venture attached to it. For example, www.libertyaid.org is a publishing website of Christian Ministries Trust. A trust should start with the name **Christian** and end with **Trust** in most cases. The trust can have other names in between like Ministries in this case. Why? Because the name of the trust is for others that are accustomed to and find these words acceptable, to communicate that this trust will be like a church to them. Doing this, your passage will be made easier while still being accurate.

• People need to understand that the Common Law Irrevocable Ecclesiastical Trust is the contract on Earth to sign your soul to God.

ADDRES

• This is a critical part and must be done correctly. Get an office with a low rental prices in a building, with multiple offices if possible. It must be a mailing address that is zoned commercially or industrially. It cannot be zoned residentially. This means no home address. A banker's software tells them whether this is a home address and they don't lend to home based businesses.

• When you are first starting out, if you just cannot find a way to get a commercial address, even by getting creative and asking someone you know who has a commercial address if they will "rent" you a part of their space, then start with the home address. BUT, it will only get

  you so far in regards to credit tiers. But at least you will be starting now, rather than doing nothing and going nowhere.

• When you do get your commercial address, you will have to change your address with the IRS, Secretary of State, Google and everywhere else that has your business address.

EIN

• Every business type needs to have an EIN to operate in commerce, open a bank account and own assets.

• An EIN is a unique identification number that is assigned to a business entity so that they can be identified by the Internal Revenue Service.

PHONE NUMBER

• This is a critical point. No mistakes allowed. There must be a landline at the office address in the name of the business. To get the phone number you need to use the EIN.

411 LISTING

• Your landline must be registered with 411. This is surprisingly difficult to do in many cases. Currently there is a website hack that gets it done for free immediately: http://www.listyourself.net

• After you list your business call and check to make sure it is listed.

• There are many other services that list businesses to assist with putting your business literally on the map. Start with Google maps and add a missing business to the map. After you have added the business then claim it and give the information to list your business. They will send you mail with a code to claim the business. Google is the biggest information agent on earth so listing with them lists with many, many other places too: www.google.com/maps

• Add the business to YellowPages, SuperPages and many more. I suggest getting 100+ business listings on Fiverr for $5-$20. This normally takes days, but you can outsource it for a few dollars and save a lot of time. You must do the following MANUALLY and are HIGHLY SUGGESTED: Google, Acxiom, Apple Maps, Bing, Citygrid, Facebook, Factual, Foursquare, Infogroup/ExpressUpdate, Localeze, Superpages, Yahoo, YP, Yelp.

EMAIL

• The email for the business must match the name of the business and website.

• For example if your business name is Don Kilam and its URL is www.donkilam.com then the email must have that extension from the website address. So the email for the business could be: support@donkilam.com. In other words, no Gmail, MSN, Yahoo or anything else.

• Companies like HostGator can help you get a URL address and an email address to match. There are other choices, HostGator is my go to, especially because they have great customer support for the website.

BANK ACCOUNT

• It is critical to open the bank account for this venture *as soon as possible*.

• Age of a corporation matters in corporate credit. Age of a corporation is determined by the date one opens a bank account for the business not the date it was incorporated.

• That is why shelf corporations are a hoax.

• At this point the best bank is Chase Bank, though any bank will do. This is my preference and doesn't relate to how much credit you can build. But, if you have good personal credit, getting one of the Chase Ink cards while signing personally can really jump start your business credit. More on this point, regarding vendor accounts, later.

DUN AND BRADSTREET NUMBER

• Now it is time to get a business credit number that tracks the credit of the business. You will do this by calling Dun and Bradstreet to get this business credit number or register online: www.dnb.com

• Dun & Bradstreet is a corporation that offers information on commercial credit as well as reports on businesses. Most notably, Dun & Bradstreet is recognizable for its Data Universal Numbering System (D.U.N.S.) numbers; these generate business information reports for more than 100 million companies around the globe.

• You do not need to pay Dun & Bradstreet to get this number. Do not get their monthly service, ever. It might take a 4-5 weeks to get the number, but that is okay. You don't need it before then anyway. Get this as soon as you get all the other points for starting a business completed.

• One item is to do an **update** of your business information on Dun and Bradstreet when you get your number from them. It is called iUpdater and you can get someone in chat to point you there. **Do an update only once every 6 months.** You will be giving Dunn & Bradstreet information that tells them you are a credit worthy company. Think of it as an estimate in favor of your business. Accounting information can be estimated, this is an estimate in favor of your business.

GOOGLE MAPS

• Go to Google Maps. Find your address of your business. If it is not currently listed on Google Maps, get it listed. Simply search "List my business on Google Maps" inside Google's search engine and they'll walk you through the process.

• The next step is to claim that map listing. That is usually done via postcard sent to the address listed. Once you receive the letter, enter the code as instructed in the letter and Google Maps will instantly list your business officially so anyone can see it, including the bankers.

SOCIAL MEDIA PRESENCE

• At the very minimum, make a Facebook page. Update posts to it daily at least. This and YouTube should be an easy and free way to market your business. This is the minimum, you can get creative and find other free ways to put your business out there so it has a presence online. The better see it, including the bankers.

• Employees – needs to be more than 10. Use 11, 12 or 13.

• Square Footage – employee times 2000 square feet. Example: 13 employees gets 26000 square feet.

• Income – Updating income will not be done upon receipt of your number or at the 6 month mark unless Dunn & Bradstreet calls. All other data points are updated in iUpdater upon receipt of your Dunn & Bradstreet number.

• When you do update your income, you will input a little more than $2 million but not much more at all, for example, $2,100,000. You may not be able to input this income amount and have to upload or type in a full financial statement here that adds up to $2.1 million in income.

• Get ready after your first year mark and fill in all other fields in the financial data on iUpdater.

• If Dun & Bradstreet calls, always tell them the four data points: income, square footage, employees and years in business. Keep your information consistent on phone and on paper. Dunn & Bradstreet corroborates your data points, this is considered a third party verification. This can no longer be done without tax records so this may not work but if it does, this is the information to put in. Mainly this is the minimum number you put for income on applications for credit if nothing else. **This will be covered in detail in the video.**

• Years in Business – 2 years. Just type this but it may not work for harder to get creditors, but it helps get your initial accounts.

You have come to the END OF THE INITIAL LAYING OF A FOUNDATION FOR A CREDIT READY CORPORATION.

Now that you have started your business correctly to access credit, you are prepared to start building your business credit.

Let's go over some strategy that no other corporate credit programs talk about before we move on to the next step.

First of all, building corporate credit should be done for something you are passionate about doing for years to come. You are going to build a service and you should find joy in what you do serving others. Since you have to go through all the steps of building a business then go ahead and make your business all about what you love to do in serving others.

That means make a part of this business a service, probably management as a part of the service. Why Services And Not Products? Because it is harder for a lender to know exactly how big a service business is, compared to being a product manufacturer.

Therefore you can get much better corporate credit if you are in the service industry. Even if you are in products, have a service as an adjunct to your products.

You're soon to have a thriving business and good corporate credit when you finish this process.

This is a key point as to why you want an ongoing business. 100% PROFIT HACK: What if you were to use this corporate credit to donate all of the credit to a trust?

Nice enough, this legal. You'll start another trust, or C Corp, and have it ready with a bank account to transfer to, because all you really need to do is to give your website a new bank account and routing number. The rest can remain the same.

Notice Regarding Social Security Numbers Even though an application asking for credit may have a space for a social security number, never fill in a social security number.

Net Term Accounts & Credit Scores The common first step in building the credit of this corporation is to get Net term accounts with businesses that report to Dun and Bradstreet.

Unlike personal credit, corporate credit is reported via a Paydex score from Dun & Bradstreet with a scale of 0 – 100. 80 is the minimum credit score needed for corporate credit. At 80 you pay the terms of your agreement on time. Above 80, you pay ahead of your agreed time. Less than 80 and you are paying late.

Corporate credit scores are simply about how fast you pay bills. Now these Net terms accounts are about getting credit that needs to be paid back in however many days it says after the word Net. Net 30 you must pay within 30 days. Net 10 you must pay within 10 days. The focus should be on starting at least (3) Net 30 accounts and (4) Net accounts all together, though (5) is added insurance.

This area of Net 30 accounts is always a moving target. Many companies will give credit to new companies but very few report to Dun & Bradstreet. You only want the ones that report to Dun & Bradstreet. No other vendor accounts will help build corporate credit. Part of your work is finding these accounts.

Some longtime leaders in this industry and still doing this type of accounting are the following vendors:
- www.grainger.com
- www.quill.com
- www.seton.com
- www.uline.com

IMPORTANT: This a very important piece of the puzzle that is always moving. If you ever find a Net terms account that reports to Dun &

Bradstreet email me immediately at support@malikkilam.com and we will update this list + give you a special finder's fee bonus!

Now that you have found these accounts what do you do? You want to make a purchase of just over $100 with each one and then click the bill me option at checkout. Pay the day the bill comes in the mail, with a check whenever possible, but they take payments over the phone too.

The most important thing is to be early in payments! In each successive month you must make another purchase from each of your Net terms vendors but these purchases can be for any amount over $50. Sometimes these accounts can take 30, 60 or 90 days to report, although usually they are fast. Call and ask them to report if it has been 30 days and they haven't reported yet.

After your credit applications are approved at (3) Net 30 terms creditors and you make 3 months of successful on-time payments in a row, your company will have a Paydex score of 80.

CREDIT HACK: An alternate choice for those with a good or great personal credit scores, is to get as many accounts as you want with a personal guarantee. This simply means that you are signing up for these credit accounts with your person AND business.

Once you are reporting with your business you can remove the personal guarantee. While this is not necessary it saves a bunch of money and time. It saves money because you will use these cards for your regular dayto-day purchases.

Whereas normally you would be forced to pay for products from the Net 30 account at the store, instead of using it for ANY purchase you want.

For example, I ordered a box of laundry detergent and toilet paper from one of my net 30 accounts at a higher price than I would have paid elsewhere.

These 3 opening accounts will be credit cards. These are the 3 types of credit cards to get if your personal credit is good enough that report to your business score and some report to your personal score too. All the rest of the accounts you get from here on out you won't get with a personal guarantee.

Each one has different card options so pick the one you can get and has the perks you like. If you go this route make sure you get the Chase and Capital One cards first.

In fact, you can get two of the Chase or Capital One cards instead of the Amex or Citi cards.

Get a total of 3 credit cards from this group with a personal guarantee, no more:
• Chase Ink
• Capital One Spark
• American Express Business
• Citi Business How Do You Know You Got A Paydex Score Of 80? Sign up with CreditSignal by Dun & Bradstreet, which is a free service. It will keep you updated as to how the score is doing. One of the most common denial reasons for any credit at any level is your company information does not match somewhere.

On Dun & Bradstreet it says 124 Long Street #33 and on your application it says 124 Long Street Number 33. T

hey won't approve your account unless all this information matches EXACTLY, all the time. To get your registered address, pull up the USPS approved address for your location and always use that. Sign up to get a service called NAV. It costs about $65 quarterly and gives you monthly updates to your personal and business credit. It also gives alerts during the month in between reporting. Get a business credit reporting subscription for the year from Experian, it costs under $200 and updates every day. You will be very up to date about your accounts that report to Experian. Not every vendor that reports does its reporting to both Dun & Bradstreet and Experian so you need both reports to see if how your corporate credit is going so you know when to take the next step or if a problem comes up you see it and cure it right away

: Becoming Credit Worthy Now that your company is viewed as a worthy credit risk, it is time to continue up the credit ladder. Once you have 3 accounts that have reported payment experiences you can move on to the next list of accounts to apply for. Many of these have Net 30 terms to start and some companies have upgrades to their vendor accounts that are better than net 30 terms.

NOTE: Leave the social security number space and the rest of the personal guarantee blank if they have a space for a personal guarantee. Many of these are applications you print, fill out and then fax into the company. Google these items exactly as these are the names of the exact type of accounts to start with to get the application. A few are online applications:

- Amazon.com - Business Pay In Full Credit Line
- Lowes.com - Accounts Receivable
- Chevron/Texaco – Chevron Texaco Business Card ($100 initial fee on the card for signing up)
- JC Penny – JC Penny Commercial (fax)
- Office Depot/Max – Business Credit Account

You must make at least $100 in purchases for these accounts to report the payment experience initially, $50 minimum thereafter usually. Once all of these companies have reported your payment experiences you can move on to the next tier of credit available. You are going to need to use these accounts every month so they report. And they are going to need to be paid on time or early. Only make one payment per month with all your accounts. But make your payment early every month. This is critical to having excellent credit.

Upgrading Your Credit Worthiness Once you have at least one payment experience reporting from each of the previously mentioned accounts you will move on to the next tier in credit applications. The next group of corporate credit accounts are store credit that is useful like office supply stores such as, if you didn't get Grainger and Uline accounts because you used the credit card hack go get those accounts and purchase at least $100 worth from them on your first order. These two accounts report and ship extremely fast. They are great credit builder accounts you can't miss.

NOTE: Remember to always spend at least $100 for each new account you have so it reports that account ASAP on your credit report.
Pay on time or early, of course. This is a list of next level vendors to make an application for credit once all of the previous vendors from this package have reported their payment experiences to the credit reports (Get the lowest tier card or credit line available if they have multiple choices for account types:
- Walmart
- Home Depot Commercial
- Sears Commercial One
- Tractor Supply
- Macy's
- Staples
- Speedway
- BP Small Business Fleet
- Hardware Express
- Gemplars -
Wells Fargo Secured Credit Card (not for trusts)

On personal credit reports the amount of inquiries matters to the score. For business credit many inquiries are expected and have no negative bearing on your business credit score. It is a natural and expected for a business to try and access credit. Dealing with business credit is a change in how you were taught to think of credit from dealing with your person's credit.

Feel free to apply to as many places as you think might accept your application for credit that report to Dun & Bradstreet.

Email To Creditors How do you find out if a potential credit provider is one that reports to Dun and Bradstreet and that you will qualify for? The best way to answer this question is via email to start.

Write each potential creditor an email with all of your information in the email. Example Email: Remember to follow up with every credit denial with a phone call or email to find out what your company was denied and how it was lacking so you can reapply when your company does qualify.

For this part of credit building try to get a total of 10 minimum accounts, but preferably 15 would be best. After you have this round of accounts reporting it is time to contact each company and ask to have the credit limit raised and in the case of gas cards or others that give store credit cards that have upgrades to Visa or MasterCard, then you want to ask for the upgrade to these cards. Your requests may not be granted, but some will be.

Lines of Credit w/o Personal Guarantee

All this work up until this point has led to you getting you access to the most important credit of all, credit cards and lines of credit with no personal guarantee. We are not there yet but we are getting very close. This stop on the credit building process will put those cards within reach. We still have to do a few thing to make it possible. It usually takes a minimum of 3 years to get credit cards and lines of credit with no personal guarantee. This should be the last tier of credit before making that possible. The next tier is much like previous tiers in that you need to use the credit for it to report. Once you have at least 10 credit lines reporting payment experiences on your credit reports its time to move on to getting more lines of credit with these creditors and as always get the lowest tier of card they offer to start with (even though you may apply to all of them you may only get some accounts approved but get as many as you can):

- AutoZone
- Staples
- Best Buy
- Shell Fleet Card

- BP Small Business Fleet
- Sinclair Business Card
- Exxon/Mobil Fleet
- Ally Car Financial
- Racetrac
- Sam's Club
- Fuelman

As always after each part in the credit building process you want to get in touch with all your creditors and ask them to raise your credit line amount and/or upgrade to a better card or account type if they offer one.

After this tier of credit accounts are all applied for, paid for and they report; it's very important to take this step. Truly this is its own mini-step within a step as there are quite a few cards on this list from the start that have upgraded accounts you can get at this point. In fact, wait until these upgraded accounts report until moving on to the next step.

Unsecured Credit Cards After 60-120 Days Now it is time to get into the real useful parts of corporate credit and why you put all this time and effort into this process. This was all to get unsecured credit cards from Visa, MasterCard and the like. These are cards that can be used outside the vendors' stores and used anywhere for anything, just like any Visa or MasterCard. This tier of the process focuses on getting unsecured credit cards as fast as possible and as much of it as possible and here is where you start to get into that credit. If you used the initial hack to get your Capital One Spark, Chase Ink, etc.; this is the time to ask and see if they will remove the personal guarantee on the cards you already have. You may get cards released from the personal guarantee and sometimes they may not take the personal guarantee off.

Either way, speak to them on the phone about what further steps you need to take to get the credit where it needs to be. What steps need to be taken? Take notes and get those steps done as soon as possible. Whenever you will apply for any of these cards remember as always to never ever write your social security number on any forms even if there is a space for it. At this level of credit card you will want to get store credit cards with a MasterCard or Visa logo. All the information of employees, income, square footage and years in business all will match on applications what you put into Dun & Bradstreet when you updated your information there. That is what the lenders look at to see if it matches so make sure you stay consistent. You may have gotten a couple of these in your last round of credit applications or you may have found you did not qualify. Now you will qualify once all these accounts are reporting.

Bank Unsecured Credit Cards Here is the step where we get some bank unsecured credit cards. One leg up to getting these cards and can be done now or immediately upon opening your bank account, is to get a secured business line of credit. This means if you deposit a large sum in a bank account of say $10,000 or more you can use this money to get a secured line of credit for your business. Like getting a secured business credit card, a secured business line of credit helps get you get a history with the bank and on your credit report of paying back your lines of credit. Keep asking your bank to flip to an unsecured line of credit from your secured line of credit as your overall business credit improves. Now that you've set everything up to get unsecured business credit cards with no personal liability and unsecured lines of credit, you want to begin to ask for this credit where you currently bank. Don't ask before this point! But now is the time to go in and ask. Sit down and turn your banker into your advocate and just ask for as much credit as they feel comfortable extending, whatever that credit limit is on the business credit card they'll give you, if you don't have one already with them from prior steps. For example, if you already have a Chase Ink card and you bank there, then ask for another Chase business card too, i.e. get another card with them. If your bank(s) approve your applications then wait until these new accounts report. After they report you want to ask for credit cards elsewhere. Remember that it doesn't matter how many inquiries you have on your account so go ahead and try to get as much as you can. Just go for cards with no annual fees and for lines of credit that have low fees and only lines of credit you will actually use after getting an initial one or two. And keep in mind there are many ways to use lines of credit. Upgrade that secured cards from Wells Fargo to unsecured if they let you and if you decided to get that card, and remember they don't give that credit card to trusts. In fact, Wells Fargo never gives any credit to any trusts, keep that in mind.. Lines of credit can then be built higher and higher as time goes on. For example, for a real estate investor with a line of credit they need only to write a check off that line of credit to purchase real estate, cash sale and fast. That means much deeper discounts on real estate investments and once initial fees are paid on a line of credit you don't pay again each time you use the line of credit, except the pay back of interest and principle of course. Another important part of this level of credit building is leasing a car and that can be done with Ally Financial or Ford Commercial. It is better to lease a car than own one, since the bank really owns it anyway and you are only financing the time you use the car on a lease not the entire value as in a sale of a car. Leases are usually half the cost of purchasing a car. And you need great credit to lease a car. NOTE: Ask a car salesman how they own their vehicles, most will say they lease it.

MONTH 6b: Going Beyond The Material No other credit building information goes beyond this point and most don't even come close to this level of understanding. KEEP IN MIND THERE ARE NO LIMITS TO CORPORATE CREDIT, THE ONLY LIMIT IS YOUR MIND. At this point you understand, you can have all you need with this information. But how to maximize the value of this information? A Bulletproof Trust. When you can find others with the same information and have demonstrated the outcomes, they will show you that they have built a business with corporate credit. Now, there is even more that can be done. For example, when you find a couple of other trustworthy business owners like yourself you can begin to do business with each other in several ways. Keep in mind that accounting information comes in two types, actual and estimated. Rarely are the files noted as such either way though the words pro forma mean estimated on accounting files. Even when accounting information is asked for in applications for credit and other places, it does not say to provide actual or estimated. How can trustworthy business owners work together? They can help each other with great accounts on their business credit. They could add the other business to certain credit cards with high balances as guarantors for those cards and then get great credit cards from this sharing or simply up their current lines of credit they have. These trustworthy owners of businesses with great credit could work out contracts for services. A service could be depositing $5,000 into each-others bank accounts every day in order to generate revenue and a good bank rating which is a hidden rating that banks use to judge a company's credit worthiness. These trustworthy business owners could sign a multi-year contract with one another. For example, if a property management services company were to contract to provide services to a real estate investment firm for 10 years for $10 million it could then go to a bank for a factor loan off that contract for say 10% - 15% of the contract value. That would be a line of credit for $1 – $1.5 million for say new equipment or anything really. The real trick at this level is contracting with one another to further the goals of getting the highest credit limits on credit cards and lines of credit available. Make sure you are doing what is right for all business owners in their credit life cycle of the business. This is all about helping others as well as yourself.

CLICK THE LINK BELOW FOR ACCESS TO THE UNICORPORATED BUSINESS TRUST!

https://drive.google.com/file/d/1jBYkY2ybPMY84XPRqgyrUTTagmrmbSTO/view?usp=sharing

NET 30 VENDORS TO BUILD BUSINESS CREDIT

Finding net-30 vendors that report to the business credit bureaus may seem like a lot of hard work. But there are several common, easy-to-apply-for vendors that report to the major bureaus. Follow our guide to find the right set of vendors to build your business credit.

Net-30 Vendors Who Report to Dun & Bradstreet

Dun & Bradstreet is arguably the most important business credit bureau when it comes to establishing and building business credit. To help you build your business credit profile, you should consider setting up net-30 starter accounts with these companies:

Uline

Uline.com is our first pick because this company carries so many useful products meant to help businesses in particular. Their customer service is wonderful. When we called them, they immediately picked up the phone (no automated recording system to have to deal with).

Uline reports to Dun & Bradstreet on the first of each month. Setting up a net-30 account with them is super easy.

Follow these steps:

1. **Call them** and tell them you're a small business that wants to set up a net-30 account.
2. **Give them your business name, billing and shipping address, and business telephone number.**
3. **Place your first order** with them (there is no minimum or maximum amount).

Quill

Quill.com is another option for a starter business that wants to establish trade lines with Dun & Bradstreet. This company sells office supplies, cleaning agents, health care and safety supplies, as well as tools and breakroom supplies.

The company does not automatically approve new businesses for net-30 accounts. You first have to build your credit with Quill first, which can take you a month or two before you qualify for credit terms. Once approved for a Quill credit account, you'll need to maintain that account for 90 to 120 days before they will start reporting your account to Dun & Bradstreet.

Follow these steps to set-up a net-30 account with Quill:

1. **Visit their website and place a prepaid order over $45.** This will establish your account with them.
2. Place a **minimum of two more orders** in your first month (over $45).
3. **Place larger orders more frequently** during month two (they recommend you place at least a $100 order, per week).
4. **Place even larger orders** during month three. This will get you in good with their credit department.

5. **Ask them to report to Dun & Bradstreet after month three.** Assuming your payment history is good, you'll likely be approved.

Office Depot/OfficeMax

Office Depot/OfficeMax is an office supply company that operates all over the United States. They sell computers, printers, software, supplies, and more. They used to offer net-30 accounts; however, now they've switched to net-20 accounts. They report to Dun & Bradstreet monthly.

To set up a net-20 account with Dun & Bradstreet, follow these steps:

1. **Visit their Business Services website** at **https://business.officedepot.com**.
2. **Click the blue "Get Started" button** to the right of the login section.
3. **Follow the prompts** to provide your information and click submit.
4. **Wait for a sales representative to contact you**, and they will open up a new business account.
5. **Wait for your net-20 account to be approved** (approximately 24-48 hours).

Grainger

Grainger is a company that specializes in industrial solutions and sells abrasives, HVAC and refrigeration components, motors, lighting, furniture, fasteners, office supplies, outdoor equipment, and so much more. They offer over 1.5 million products. They also offer small businesses net-30 accounts to pay for those products. Grainger regularly reports to Dun & Bradstreet.

Here's how to get a net-30 account with Grainger:

1. **Open a new business account** by clicking on the "Register Now" link at the top right of the Grainger **homepage**.
2. **Select "For Business Use"** and continue filling in the required information to proceed. New accounts are usually set up within two business days. You will receive an email with the new account number once the account is ready to be used.
3. **Email a request for open account billing** to graingercredit@grainger.com. Please include your account number, the signature of the Owner or Officer of the company, and a note that you understand Grainger's payment terms are Net 30 days from the invoice date and that you will pay invoices within these terms.

HD Supply

HD Supply sells appliances, fitness and exercise equipment, healthcare supplies, janitorial, linens, paint and supplies, office supplies, food service equipment, HVAC, window coverings, etc. This is a great company to partner with because they report to Dun and Bradstreet, offer net-30 terms, and have products that fit nearly any business's needs.

Here's how to get a net-30 account with HD Supply:

1. **Apply for a net-30** credit account at **https://hdsupplysolutions.com/s/credit_application**.
2. **Click the HD Supply Facilities Maintenance Credit Application link**. This will take you to their online credit application form.
3. **Fill in the form** with your business information and click submit.
4. **Wait for approval** (approximately 24-48 hours).
5. **Begin placing your orders** once your account has been approved.

Summa Office Supplies

Summa Office Supplies sells pencils, pens, folders, tape, and just about everything else your office needs. Their customer service is friendly and helpful, and they offer net-30 accounts for small businesses (even new and unestablished businesses).

Before you apply for a net-30, you should know they operate on a **tier 1** and **tier 2** credit system. This means when you open up an account with them, they will automatically put you into the tier 1 category. This category will require you to prepay for your purchases for six months while you establish a history with them. During this tier 1 phase, they will report trade lines to Equifax Small Business, **not** Dun & Bradstreet.

After six months has elapsed, you'll qualify for tier 2 and then receive net-30 credit terms. When you reach tier 2, the company will start reporting to Dun & Bradstreet monthly.

Here's how to apply:

1. **Visit Summa's website** at https://summaofficesupplies.com/.
2. **Click on "Create an Account"** in the top right corner.
3. **Fill in your business information** and click submit.
4. **Place your first prepaid order**.
5. **Keep placing regular orders** to build your business credit with Summa and Equifax Small Business.
6. **Place a $300+ order after six months** has elapsed and **click on "pay later."**
7. **Get approval within 24 hours** (you'll now be qualified for 30 day invoicing).

Prerequisites: You must file with the Secretary of State, have a DUNS number, and a business phone number with a 411 directory listing.

Net-30 Vendors Who Report to Experian Business

Experian Business is another business credit bureau that is often reported to, and one where creditors often pull your credit report to determine your creditworthiness. It is advisable to have some established lines of credit with this credit reporting agency. Here are some vendors to help you establish business credit with Experian Business.

Uline

Uline.com is our first pick again because this company carries so many useful products, their customer service is fantastic, and they're extremely easy to work with.

Earlier, we mentioned that Uline reports to Dun & Bradstreet, but they also report to Experian on the first of each month also. As mentioned, setting up a net-30 account with them is super easy.

Follow these steps:

1. **Call them** and tell them you're a small business that wants to set up a net-30 account.
2. **Give them your business name, billing and shipping address, and business telephone number.**

3. **Place your first order** with them (there is no minimum or maximum amount).

Strategic Network Solutions

Strategic Network Solutions is a supplier for Dell Computers, AVG, various hardware and software companies (e.g., PCM, TigerDirect), and they provide information technology services solutions to over 3000 clients globally. They also report to Experian Business and CreditSafe on the last day of every month.

Here's how to apply for a net-30 account with them:

1. **Visit the Strategic Network Solutions** website at https://stntsol.com/.
2. **Click on "Register"** in the top right corner.
3. **Fill in your business information** and click submit.
4. **Choose a $75 downloadable product.**
5. **Click "Bill My Net 30"** at checkout.
6. **Pay within 30 days.**

Crown Office Supplies

Crown Office Supplies offers net-30 credit accounts, and **they report to all the major credit bureaus**. They work well with new businesses trying to establish their business credit.

This company sells office supplies and school supplies along with mobile accessories and sanitation supplies. The assortment of products is good, they offer **great sales**, and they're **continually updating their inventory**.

Setting up a net-30 account is easy with them:

1. **Visit their website** at https://crownofficesupplies.com/.
2. **Click on "APPLY FOR BUSINESS NET30"** (located just above their logo).

3. **Fill out the application**.
4. **Receive an email**, call, and text letting you know you've been approved.
5. **Login to your account and complete your annual membership**. Membership is $99 but will be reported to all the business credit bureaus. It may be waived if you have an excellent business credit score.
6. **Make a purchase**, and be sure to click on "net-30" at checkout.
7. **Pay your invoice** within 30 days.

Net-30 Vendors Who Report to Equifax Small Business

Equifax Small Business is another business credit reporting agency that is important to maintain a good business credit profile with. This company is less reported to than Dun & Bradstreet and Experian Business. However, some companies will check your Equifax Small Business report to determine creditworthiness, so you'll want to make sure your report is clean.

Crown Office Supplies

Crown Office Supplies offers net-30 credit accounts, and **they report to all the major business credit reporting agencies**. They help new businesses establish business credit.

This company sells mainly office supplies. The assortment of products is decent, and they discount items frequently.

Setting up a net-30 account with Crown Office Supplies is easy:

1. **Visit their website** at https://crownofficesupplies.com/.

2. **Click on** "APPLY FOR BUSINESS NET30" (located just above their logo).
3. **Fill out the application**.
4. **Receive an email**, call, and text letting you know you've been approved.
5. **Login to your account** and **complete your annual membership**. Membership is $99 but will be reported to all the business credit bureaus. It may be waived if you have an excellent business credit score.
6. **Make a purchase**, and be sure to click on net-30 at checkout.
7. **Pay your invoice** within 30 days.

Summa Office Supplies

Summa Office Supplies sells office supplies and more. Their customer service is great, and they will extend net-30 accounts to new businesses that have yet to establish business credit.

Before you apply for a net-30, you should know they operate on a **tier 1** and **tier 2** credit system. This means when you open up an account with them, they will automatically put you into the tier 1 category. This category will require you to prepay for your purchases for six months while you establish a history with them. During this tier 1 phase, they will report trade lines to **Equifax Small Business**, not Dun & Bradstreet. After six months has elapsed, you'll qualify for tier 2 and then receive net-30 credit terms. When you reach tier 2, the company will start reporting to Dun & Bradstreet monthly.

Here's how to apply:

1. **Visit Summa's website** at https://summaofficesupplies.com/.
2. **Click on** "Create an Account" in the top right corner.
3. **Fill in your business information** and click submit.
4. **Place your first prepaid order.**

5. **Keep placing regular orders** to build your business credit with Summa and Equifax Small Business.
6. **Place a $300+ order after six months** has elapsed and **click on "pay later."**
7. **Get approval within 24 hours** (you'll now be qualified for 30 day invoicing).

LEARN MOOR ABOUT THE POWER OF BUSINESS CREDIT WITH MONICA MAINE
CLICK THE LINK BELOW FOR THE POWER POINT PRESENTATION FOR YOU!
https://drive.google.com/file/d/1p5x3QDtJViUrJHYiOO8REzpo6N
OQ-loz/view?usp=sharing

Importance of Holding Companies

A holding company is a firm that doesn't have any actually operations, but rather only has investments in other firms. Most businesses are organized as operating companies, meaning they manufacture items or provide services. Essentially, a holding company invests in operating companies that actually produce goods or offer services. When a company has its own operations and also owns other companies, it's known as a parent company rather than a holding company. Here is an overview of holding and parent companies, including how they are similar to and different from each other.

A basic introduction to holding companies and how they work

Whether you are beginning to invest in securities issued by corporations—such as common stocks, preferred stocks, or corporate bonds—or you are considering investing in your own business, you may encounter something known as a holding company.

Many of the most successful companies in the world are holding companies. Learn about the overall structure, purpose, and benefits of holding companies, along with examples of how they work.

Definition of a Holding Company

The Balance

A holding company is a company that doesn't have any operations, activities, or other active business itself. Instead, the holding company owns assets.

These assets can be shares of stock in other corporations, limited liability companies, limited partnerships, private equity funds, hedge funds, public stocks, bonds, real estate, song rights, brand names, patents, trademarks, copyrights—virtually anything that has value.

For example, one of the most respected blue-chip stocks in the world, Johnson & Johnson, is really a holding company.[1] The firm itself doesn't actually produce anything.

Instead, Johnson & Johnson holds ownership stakes in more than 250 separate businesses.[2] The ownership isn't much different from the way you might own shares of different businesses through a brokerage account. Johnson & Johnson's businesses are grouped under three major headings—consumer healthcare, medical devices, and pharmaceuticals—but each of the subsidiaries is a stand-alone company with its own offices, bank accounts, and manufacturing facilities.[3] They are located in countries around the world and staffed by local employees.

At the top, Johnson & Johnson's stockholders elect a board of directors to protect their interests. That board is responsible for (among many things) determining the dividend policy and hiring the CEO. The CEO, in turn, hires their direct subordinates. This group of people collectively has the power to determine the CEOs and key executives at the subsidiary companies under Johnson & Johnson's control. The parent holding company supports the subsidiaries by lowering the cost of capital due to its overall strength.

For example, Johnson & Johnson can issue bonds at rock-bottom rates, then lend money to its subsidiaries at rates the subsidiaries couldn't get if they were stand-alone enterprises. This reduces interest expenses and, in turn, increases both returns on equity and returns on assets.

A Sample Holding Company

To better understand the concept of a holding company, imagine that you and a friend decide to invest together. You create a new company called Blue Sky Holding Company, Inc. After you file the paperwork with the secretary of state, you issue 1 million shares of stock at $10 per share, raising $10 million in fresh cash. You and your friend elect a board of directors. That board hires you as a CEO.

The next day, you and your friend start investing the $10 million. As Blue Sky Holding Company, you do several things:

- You incorporate a new business called Frozen Treats of America, LLC. It is 100% owned by Blue Sky Holding Company. You contribute $1.5 million in cash to the business, hire a manager to run it, and open a restaurant franchise that's expected to earn $170,000 in profit before taxes.

- You have Blue Sky Holding Company open a brokerage account with a discount brokerage firm. You deposit $3 million in cash into the account and buy a collection of high-quality, blue-chip stocks. You expect these stocks to generate $150,000 in pre-tax dividends each year.

- You start a new company called Southworth Hospitality, LLC, which is 100% owned by Blue Sky Holding Company. You contribute $2 million of Blue Sky's cash and have this new subsidiary borrow another $2 million from a bank, giving it a capitalization structure of $4 million in assets: $2 million in liabilities and $2 million in book value. The company will use the $4 million in cash to buy a hotel franchise, which is expected to generate $320,000 in pre-tax profits after interest expense and all other costs. This debt is not guaranteed by the holding company, because you decided only to allow non-recourse liabilities in case the hotel isn't successful. That means that if the subsidiary goes bankrupt, you are only on the hook for the equity Blue Sky has invested in it.

- You buy $2 million worth of tax-free municipal bonds, which you believe will generate $100,000 in annual interest income.

- You use $500,000 to buy gold coins and silver bullion.

- You park the final $1 million at the local bank in institutional money market funds that pay 2% interest, generating $20,000 in pre-tax interest income each year.

Holding Company Financial Statements

The consolidated balance sheet of this holding company is going to show $12 million in assets, $2 million in debt, and a $10 million net worth, or book value. The balance sheet appears as follows:

Blue Sky Holding Company, Inc.—Balance Sheet

- Frozen Treats of America, LLC—100% ownership ($1.5 million assets, no liabilities)
- Southworth Hospitality, LLC—100% ownership ($4 million assets, $2 million liabilities, $2 million net worth)
- Tax-free municipal bonds ($2 million assets, no liabilities)

- Blue-chip common stocks in brokerage account ($3 million assets, no liabilities)
- Bank balances ($1 million assets, no liabilities)
- Gold and silver reserves ($500,000 assets, no liabilities)

The holding company income statement is going to show $760,000 in operating income (profit before taxes from all the holdings). That would be a 7.6% return on equity because the $760,000 income divided by the $10 million net worth is 7.6%. It would be a 6.3% return on assets because $760,000 divided by $12 million in assets (which includes borrowed cash) is 6.3%.

How to Think About a Holding Company

As the CEO of Blue Sky Holding Company, Inc., what do you actually *do*?

Because Blue Sky is a holding company, you have no day-to-day role in any of the investments. Each is run by its own management team. Your job is executive oversight, support, setting risk management parameters, and putting the right people in the right places to align with corporate strategy.[4] When subsidiaries pay out dividends to Blue Sky, that money can be invested in other opportunities.

You aren't going to be making ice cream cones at your restaurant franchise. That is the job of Frozen Treats of America, LLC, a wholly-owned subsidiary with its own employees, managers, financial statements, contracts, and bank loans. Instead, you are going to watch the CEO of that company and make sure they hit the targets that the board expects.

The board will have expectations for both you and for the subsidiary. The expectations for you have to do with how well you can help subsidiary CEOs reach their targets, and how well you can increase profits while reducing risk.

The Benefits of the Holding Company Model

What if something horrible happened? For example, what if your hotel franchise went bankrupt? If the holding company itself didn't co-sign on the debt, it isn't liable for the loss. Instead, you would record a $2 million write-off in Blue Sky's net worth as a capital loss on your shares of Southworth Hospitality, LLC.

The holding company model protected the other assets from the loss experienced by this subsidiary. You won't lose your restaurant franchise just because the hotel franchise went bankrupt. Similarly, your holding company's stocks, bonds, gold, silver, and bank balances are all unaffected. You only lost the money you invested in that one subsidiary.

This is how large corporations protect themselves. Procter & Gamble, to give a real-world illustration, is effectively a holding company because it has different subsidiaries for different purposes. Some subsidiaries own brand names, such as Tide detergent.[5] Other, totally separate subsidiaries own the manufacturing plants that make Tide, and those manufacturers pay the brand-owning company a licensing royalty. That way, if the firm is sued, Procter & Gamble could never lose the Tide brand name. Instead, the factory or distributor would go bankrupt.

How It Works

There are two main ways through which corporations can become holding companies. One is by acquiring enough voting stock or shares in another company; hence, giving it the power to control its activities. The second way is by creating a new corporation from the ground up, and then retaining all or part of the new corporation's shares.

Although owning more than 50% of the voting stock of another firm guarantees greater control, a parent company can control the decision-making process even if it owns only 10% of its stock.

The relationship between the mother company and that of the corporations they control is called a parent-subsidiary relationship. In such a case, the mother company is known as the parent company while the organization being acquired is called a subsidiary. If the parent company controls all the voting stock of the other firm, that organization is called a wholly-owned subsidiary of the parent company.

Types of Holding Companies

1. Pure

A holding company is described as pure if it was formed for the sole purpose of owning stock in other companies. Essentially, the company does not participate in any other business other than controlling one or more firms.

2. Mixed

A mixed holding company not only controls another firm but also engages in its own operations. It's also known as a holding-operating company.

Holding companies that take part in completely unrelated lines of business from their subsidiaries are referred to as conglomerates.

3. Immediate

An immediate holding company is one that retains voting stock or control of another company, in spite of the fact that the company itself is already controlled by another entity. Put simply, it's a type of holding company that is already a subsidiary of another.

4. Intermediate

An intermediate holding is a firm that is both a holding company of another entity and a subsidiary of a larger corporation. An intermediate holding firm might be exempted from publishing financial records as a holding company of the smaller group.

Benefits of a Holding Company

1. Greater control for a smaller investment

It gives the holding company owner a controlling interest in another without having to invest much. When the parent company purchases 51% or more of the subsidiary, it automatically gains control of the acquired firm. By not purchasing 100% of each subsidiary, a small business owner gains control of multiple entities using a very small investment.

2. Independent entities

If a holding company exercises control over several companies, each of the subsidiaries is considered an independent legal entity. This means that if one of the subsidiaries were to face a lawsuit, the plaintiffs have no right to claim the assets of the other subsidiaries. In fact, if the subsidiary being sued acted independently, then it's highly unlikely that the parent company will be held liable.

3. Management continuity

Whenever a parent company acquires other subsidiaries, it almost always retains the management. This is an important factor for many owners of subsidiaries-to-be who are deciding whether to agree to the acquisition or not. The holding firm can choose not to be involved in the activities of the subsidiary except when it comes to strategic decisions and monitoring the subsidiary's performance.

That means that the managers of the subsidiary firm retain their previous roles and continue conducting business as usual. On the other hand, the holding company owner benefits financially without necessarily adding to his management duties.

4. Tax effects

Holding companies that own 80% or more of every subsidiary can reap tax benefits by filing consolidated tax returns. A consolidated tax return is one that combines the financial records of all the acquired firms together with that of the parent company. In such a case, should one of the subsidiaries encounter losses, they will be offset by the profits of the other subsidiaries. In addition, the net effect of filing a consolidated return is a reduced tax liability.

Summary

A holding company is one that individuals form for the purpose of purchasing and owning shares in other companies. By "holding" stock, the parent company gains the right to influence and control business decisions. Holding companies offer several benefits such as gaining more control at a small investment, retaining the management of the subsidiary firm, and incurring lower tax liabilities.

How to Form a Holding Company

Holding companies are formed to organize and manage a group of smaller companies. If you are a business owner or investor, you may consider forming a holding company to protect your business assets or get a more favorable tax rate.

Part 1

Creating Your Holding and Operating Companies

1

Assess your business needs. A holding company is an incorporated business that holds investments in other companies, called operating companies. The holding company does not perform any business activities other than borrowing, lending, and making investment decisions. However, the holding company loans funds or leases assets to an operating company that performs any kind of business activities. The two most common benefits of a holding company are tax reduction and asset protection. A holding company may provide a reduced tax rate by incorporating in a state with a more favorable tax structure, or it may protect company assets from loss to creditors of the operating company. Before forming a holding company you should consider your business needs and the benefits you want to achieve.

- A famous holding company in the US is Warren Buffett's Berkshire Hathaway. Berkshire Hathaway is a holding company that lends to and invests in operating companies, including GEICO and Coke.[1] The holding company can borrow at lower rates than other businesses because it has ownership in such a diverse group of businesses. At the same time, the business profits greatly from the increase in the stock value of businesses it invests in.
- A holding company may also be suited for the owner of a small business, as the holding company can provide asset protection for the high value assets of the operating company. In this way, by forming a holding and operating company, a single person can protect both their personal and business high value assets from creditors of the operations of the business.

2

Determine your business structure. There are two predominate forms for a holding company, the corporation and the Limited Liability Company or LLC. You should determine which form fits your needs, as the form you choose may affect your taxes and liability. Most small business owners choose to form an LLC holding company, as the corporation structure generally do not provide the same asset protection.[2] Consider what type of company you already have, if any, and what form of holding and operations company will suit your needs.

- If you are seeking a more favorable tax structure, you may consider forming your holding company in a separate state than the operating company. You should consult a business attorney for help setting up a company in another state.
- To maximize asset protection, you can form two LLCs, one holding and one operating company. You must create a separate entity for each, but the agent for each can be the same person - you. As long as you maintain the holding and operating companies as separate legal entities, the holding company will not be liable for debts of the operating company.

3

File a business application. You will form your holding company according to the state laws and the type of business you want to form. Whether you form an LLC or corporation, you will need to file registration with the state by giving the name of the business, the name of the business agent, and the articles of incorporation for your company. You should do this for your operating company as well as your holding company if your operating company is not already incorporated.

- Your articles of incorporation should state the purpose of your company and its objective, the names of the officers of the company, and how business decisions will be made. Update the articles of incorporation as you make business changes.

4

Create a bank account specific to your holding company. To maintain independence as separate companies, the holding company and the operating company must maintain separate bank accounts and accounting records.[3] You should open a business account specific to your holding company by providing your new company tax ID when you create the account. Deposit all of the funds you will use to

5

Fund the holding company. To start using the holding company, you should fund the company to start investing in the operating company. The wealth of your companies should be stored in the holding company, and you can loan money to the operating company to fund operations as needed.

- If your operating company was already started before the holding company, start by selling all of the valuable assets of the operating company (such as land, buildings, large equipment, intellectual property, etc) to the holding company by filing a transfer of assets.[4]

6

Keep accounting records for your transactions. As you operate your operating and holding companies, maintain accurate accounting records of the transactions that take place between your businesses. Separate accounting records are critical to maintaining legal distinction between the entities. The holding company must claim income for amounts it earns from the holding company in lease or rent revenue, so much as that amount exceeds the expense of owning the asset. You should keep records so that at the end of the year, you can account for all transfers that took place between your holding and operating companies.[5]

Part 2

Operating Your Holding and Operating Companies

1

Perform all operating activities through the operating company. Business activities are categorized as either operating, investing, or financing activities, and you must perform all operating activities through your operating company, not through your holding company. Operating activities are the sale of goods and services that drive revenue in a business, like the sale of groceries or clothing, or the sale of services such as dental work or carpet cleaning. To ensure that your holding company is never liable to creditors of the operating company, the holding company must never be involved in these operating activities.

- The phrase "piercing the corporate veil" is commonly used to describe when a holding company is held liable for the debts of an operating entity. This happens when the operations of the two companies are so intertwined, the holding company is held responsible to pay for the debts of the operating company.[6]
- All employees who perform operating functions should be employees of the operating company, and should be paid using the operating company funds.

2

Invest and finance using the holding company. The holding company can act as a lender or lessor to the operating company, so that the holding company owns the business' assets, and the operating company leases them from the holding company. Each month the operating company will pay lease expense to the holding company, providing cash flow back to the holding company. The holding company may also own land and charge rent to the operating company to use it, or loan money to the operating company and collect interest payments.

- You should aim to have most of the cash between the businesses stored with the holding company, where it can earn interest, and loan to the operating company when necessary. So long as the cash is on the holding company accounts, it is not subject to liabilities of the operating company.
- Many holding companies invest in multiple businesses, by owning stocks in multiple businesses and securing low interest using the financial security of the diverse investment. The holding company earns income on the investment growth in the smaller companies, as well as any interest or lease revenue it earns.
- Remember to always maintain separate bank accounts and records for each of the companies, so that you can track your activity and report on it.

3

File taxes and pay franchise fees. You will file two separate tax returns, one for the holding and one for the operating company. File your taxes annually, consult an accountant if you need to. You may also be required to pay state franchise fees for your companies, as well as filing any necessary reports with state business registries. Consult a business attorney if you are unsure what taxes and fees apply to your businesses

Holding companies are designed to acquire equity in other companies. However, this is not the same as buying stock in another company. Equity ownership refers to ownership in a company even if that company does not issue stock. For example, joining two other partners in the ownership of a company makes you an equity owner, regardless of whether or not stock is issued.

Stock owners are a type of equity owner. While holding companies can own assets that include stock, there are other types of equity, such as hedge funds, real estate and song rights. Holding companies deal with the ownership of almost anything of value in a business.

Why Create a Holding Company?

The main reasons that business owners consider creating a holding company are to protect assets, reap tax benefits and have control or influence over other companies.

Businesses owned entirely by holding companies can all be filed under the same tax return, saving time and money. The value of the holding company itself rises if the value of the stocks it owns in various businesses goes up. By having certain levels of equity in a business, the holding company can help dictate its direction and operations.

A holding company maintains equity in an operating company, but if the holding company does not co-sign onto the operating company's debt, it is not responsible for that debt. This can shield assets from creditors. Assets are held by the holding company, which also helps shield those assets from lawsuits and debt liabilities. The holding company is only at risk of declines in worth and capital.

Evaluate Your Needs

Because the value of a holding company lies in protecting assets and influencing other businesses, there are only specific instances in which it is worth it to create a holding company. If you want to do so, begin by evaluating your current business needs.

If you are concerned about asset protection, for example, a holding company may be of value. However, holding companies are often created for potential tax benefits. You can create an operating company and a holding company, both of which are different legal bodies, and shield the holding company from the debt of the operating company.

Register Your Company

To create your holding company, you register it in a state and provide your business name, articles of incorporation and the name of the business agent managing the operating and holding company. If you so choose, you can be the agent for both the operating and holding company.

Your articles of incorporation outline the purpose of your company, list its officers and specify the method by which business-related decisions will be made. You also need to create a bank account that is unique and specific to your holding company. The operating and holding companies must use separate bank accounts and keep track of their bank records separately.

Deposit Your Assets

The wealth that your company generates is deposited with the holding company, rather than the operating company. This money can then be lent to the operating company as needed. If your operating company is already in existence at the time that you started your holding company, you can sell your operating company's assets to the holding company to protect them.

To grow and diversify the portfolio of your holding company, you may end up choosing to invest in or acquire tangible or intangible equity in other businesses as opportunities arise.

Estate Planning & Asset Protection

We believe it very important to protect your assets from probate through estate planning which goes hand in hand with the Holding Company and Trust Corporations. Another way we believe to protect your assets on the public side would be though a special Holding Company!

The Benefits of forming an LLC in Wyoming are:

- No state taxes
- Asset protection and limited liability
- Members nor Managers are not listed with the state
- Best asset protection laws
- No citizenship requirements
- Perpetual life
- Transferability of ownership
- Ability to build credit & raise capital
- Number of owners is unlimited
- Lower startup costs- with Registered Agents of Wyoming LLC, the cost of forming an LLC is affordable.

Key benefits explained

No state taxes

There are no State taxes in Wyoming on an LLC. If you choose to form an LLC in Wyoming your company may not pay State taxes at all. Consider what you paid last year in your States income tax. If you are comparing Nevada and Wyoming for instance, Wyoming has never had a state income tax on LLCs.

Asset protection and limited liability

A properly formed LLC is recognized as a separate legal entity with its own Federal tax ID Number. The LLC is responsible for its liabilities and its debts...NOT the owners.

A Wyoming LLC offers its members and managers a high degree of protection from lawsuits. And doing business as a Wyoming limited liability company allows you to maintain your privacy while also allowing for asset protection.

Privacy allowed

An owner of a Wyoming LLC enjoys unparalleled security and privacy due to the following:

- Reporting and Disclosure obligations are minimal.
- Wyoming limited liability company ownership is not maintained on Wyoming public records.
- There is no requirement to list a manager or member for the duration of your Wyoming limited liability company (LLC).

No citizenship requirements

You do not have to be a U.S. citizen to form an LLC. You may live anywhere i the world and operate your Wyoming LLC.

You can operate your LLC and live anywhere in the world and you do not have to be a US citizen to form an LLC in Wyoming. But in order to give substance to your operation you should know about our Wyoming Address and Mail Forwarding Service and learn how use of this inexpensive option will help give "presence" to your remote business operations.

Easy to move

Wyoming has made it easy to move your existing LLC to Wyoming. Something you can not do in Nevada. That service is detailed here.

Perpetual life - unlimited duration

A limited liability company is a separate legal entity with an existence of its own and a perpetual life. Therefore, the business may continue far beyond this lifetime and into future generations.

By comparison, Sole proprietorships typically end upon the death of the owner. An LLC, however, continues indefinitely until it is dissolved. Memberships in an LLC can generally be sold, gifted or bequeathed to others.

Transferability of ownership

A sole proprietorship does not have a life apart from its owner and it may not be transferred to a third party. The LLC, however, provides an excellent vehicle for transferring ownership: Ownership may be transferred by an exchange of membership.

Ability to build credit & raise capital

Because a corporation is a separate legal entity with its own tax identification number (similar to a social security number for an individual) an LLC can build credit, borrow money and sell equity to raise capital. Most investors prefer investing in a LLC because of the limited liability and ease of transfer of the investment.

Number of owners

LLCs generally allow for single-owner on up to an unlimited number of memberships (except with S-Corporation status, there is a limit of 100 members).

Asset Protection: The Corporate Veil and Charging Orders

You can plan in such a way that increases your potential to protect your assets and property from creditor claims. This type of planning must start long before you need it, and learning about the possible ways that a business entity can help you with asset protection planning is a great place to start.

A business entity like a corporation or limited liability company (LLC) will help protect you in two ways: corporate veil protection and charging order protection. However, you must properly set up your business entity for this protection to function properly. You must also maintain your business and follow any necessary formalities as required by state law.

Table of Contents

- What Is Asset Protection?
- Starting the Asset Protection Process
- The Corporate Veil: The Basics
- Piercing the Corporate Veil
- Charging Order Protection
- The Limits of Charging Order Protection
- Other Means of Asset Protection Planning
- Planning Properly for Asset Protection

View more

What Is Asset Protection?

Many people assume that asset protection planning is just another term for "hiding" your assets from creditors, but that is not the case. Instead, asset protection operates well within the confines of the law. It is smart and completely legal.

PROPER ASSET PROTECTION

Proper asset protection will help you keep your property safe from creditors. These creditors may hold any type of debt against you, including debt from simple outstanding invoices to large civil judgments from a lawsuit.

Anyone can end up facing a lawsuit that can cost them thousands of dollars, regardless of whether or not you own your own business. Someone can easily get hurt on your property or you may cause a car accident, resulting in a costly legal battle. If your insurance company denies you coverage, you may be on the hook for the injured party's medical bills, lost wages, pain and suffering, and a lot more. Proper asset protection planning helps you avoid losing some of the most important and valuable property that you own.

Starting the Asset Protection Process

While asset protection planning is completely legal, you must initiate the process long before you actually need it. If you start moving assets after litigation starts or on the eve of trial, you are going to have problems.

Transferring assets out of your name with the intent to hinder, defraud, or delay a particular creditor is illegal. These are called "fraudulent transfers." While the term is often associated with bankruptcy, state laws have their own version of what constitutes a fraudulent transfer or fraudulent conveyance. The definitions are very similar.

Instead, you should begin planning for asset protection as soon as possible, just in case you need it. It is never too early to get the process started. Proper planning can help you keep some of your most valuable assets and protect your business as well.

The Corporate Veil: The Basics

Corporations and LLCs are separate legal entities. They can enter into contracts on their own, and they can incur debt by themselves. They also have their own legal responsibility for their actions. Due to this separate legal status, owners and shareholders are generally not liable for obligations of the corporation or LLC. Instead, their liability is limited to the investment that they have provided to the enterprise. This limited liability is often referred to as the "corporate veil."

The corporate veil protects owners' and shareholders' assets from the obligations of the company, so they are not personally liable for contracts, debts, or even lawsuits against the business.

Piercing the Corporate Veil

The liability protection that corporations and LLCs provide is not absolute. Instead, a creditor can "pierce the corporate veil" and make owners or shareholders personally liable under certain circumstances. Essentially, the creditor attempting to pierce the corporate veil will have to prove that the company is really just a shell or a sham, or that the corporation's actions were fraudulent or that particular owners acted irresponsibly.

Failing to follow corporate formalities is one of the most common reasons that creditors can pierce the corporate veil. For example, corporations have an obligation to conduct annual shareholders' and board of directors' meetings and keep minutes of these meetings. They must also issue stock and track the sale of stock. They also have reporting obligations to the state that must be met to keep their corporate status. Failing to fulfill any of these obligations may result in a claim that the corporation is not acting like a corporation and should be ignored to determine liability.

Another common pitfall is that the owners or shareholders of the company do not maintain the business separately from their own personal responsibilities. This is particularly prevalent with single-owner entities. Companies need to have a separate bank account and financial tracking system.

Failing to adhere to corporate requirements can ultimately undermine the asset protection that the corporation or LLC provides to its owners.

Charging Order Protection

While many people have heard of corporate veil protection, charging order protection is far less well-known. Charging order protection essentially offers asset protection in the opposite direction as corporate veil protection. It protects the business from legal obligations that may be created by the individual owners.

For example, imagine that your daughter has friends over to jump on the trampoline. One friend falls off and is seriously injured. Her parents sue you, and your homeowners insurance does not offer protection for trampoline accidents. That means that you must pay for the medical expenses associated with the fall on your own.

If the girl's parents get a judgment against you, they can start trying to collect through putting a lien on your home or garnishing your wages. For business owners, this can be a problem because they may try to access some of the company's assets as part of their collection efforts as well. Charging order protection cuts off the liability with the business; only you will be personally liable for the little girl's injuries. That way, your company will continue to function and be completely unaffected by your personal obligations.

Charging order protection is particularly important for businesses that have many owners or in situations where the owners may be "litigation prone" or own other businesses. In those circumstances, charging order protection helps other owners protect their investment as well. It simply would not be fair that one owner's personal liabilities would affect all of the owners..

If a creditor does get a judgment against you and tries to collect, the only thing that he or she will be able to obtain from your business is the income that you receive from it. That is, if the company gives you wages or dividends, then the creditor may be able to garnish that income. Nonetheless, the assets and income provided to other owners will remain protected thanks to charging order protection.

The Limits of Charging Order Protection

Just like corporate veil protection, charging order protection will only help you if your business is not a sham company or "alter ego" or "extension" of the owner. It may also be limited depending on the type of business entity you use. Generally, corporations offer strong charging order protection, but LLCs may not be as solid.

One of the reasons that charging order protection developed is because of the "fairness" of it. That is, other owners of a company should not be liable for your personal debt obligations merely because they own a business with you. By shielding the business, charging order protection also protects the other owners of the company. However, when there is only one owner or member of an LLC, this rationale simply does not apply.

Today, only five states provide charging order protection to single-member LLCs:
- Alaska
- South Dakota
- Nevada
- Delaware
- Wyoming

In fact, Delaware, Nevada, and Wyoming are often considered three of the friendliest states for business in the United States.

The remaining 45 states limit charging order protection to multi-member LLCs and corporations. This fact is extremely important to keep in mind if you are considering forming a new business.

Other Means of Asset Protection Planning

Developing a corporation or LLC is certainly not the only way that you can engage in asset protection planning. However, forming a business is the only means of obtaining corporate veil protection or charging order protection. Nonetheless, other asset protection tools may be used in combination with your company or separately.

Examples of other asset protection tools may include the following:

- Insurance – Many people overlook insurance as an asset protection tool, but it can be useful in protecting you from creditors. Insurance can cover both personal liabilities and business obligations, making it a reliable choice for asset protection. General liability insurance, homeowners insurance, and auto insurance are all good examples of insurance that provide a valuable asset protection service on your behalf.
- Trusts – Trusts are similar to corporations or LLCs because they are also considered separate legal entities. However, the trust must be "irrevocable" to obtain this status. Otherwise, revocable trusts are often just regarded as an extension of the trust owner. In an irrevocable trust, the assets are transferred to the trust. As the owner of the trust is no longer the owner of the property within the trust, creditors have a much harder time accessing anything in the trust. Like businesses, however, creditors can still often obtain any income derived from the trust, including most distributions.
- Exempt assets – Most states have a list of "exempt" assets. These assets are those that creditors cannot legally take. They often include things like your home, your retirement account, or your personal items (clothing, home furnishings, etc.). Putting money into these exempt assets allows you to keep the money safe from creditors. For example, some states completely exempt retirement accounts from creditor collection. By putting extra money in your retirement account, you are essentially keeping that money in a safe that creditors cannot touch. However, once you take the money out, a creditor may be able to reach it. The example also does not work if your state does not exempt retirement accounts. Many people also put additional money on their mortgage as an asset protection mechanism. This is because many states have a homestead exemption that protects your home from creditors.
- Gifts – If you no longer own the property, creditors generally have a hard time collecting it. That means that if you give gifts to others, creditors cannot go after that property either. However, it is important to note that gifting assets to others just before going to trial or filing for bankruptcy can be considered fraud—be careful!

Planning Properly for Asset Protection

Asset protection planning requires careful thought and deliberation. It may also require some creativity. Regardless of how you decide to protect your assets, you need to get the process started early for it to be most effective when you need it.

DYNASTY TRUSTS- THE MOST POWERFUL TOOL AVAILABLE TO

COMBAT THE ESTATE, GIFT, AND GENERATION SKIPPING TAXES

Introduction

On December 22, 2017, President Trump signed the Tax Cuts and Jobs Act of 2017. The 2017 Tax Cuts and Jobs Act increased the exemptions for federal estate tax, gift tax, and generation-skipping tax ("GST") to $11,180,000 per person for 2018. The exemptions are indexed for inflation. The tax rates on estates, gifts, and GST transfers is forty percent. The 2017 Tax Cuts and Jobs Act contains a sunset provision. The exemption for federal estate tax, gift tax, and GST are scheduled to revert back to $5.5 million effective January 1, 2026. As a result of the 2017 Tax Cuts and Jobs Act, individuals are presented with a number of estate planning opportunities to transfer significant amounts of wealth out of their estate without the imposition of transfer taxes. Dynasty trusts has become a popular tool to transfer taxable assets out of an individual's estate.

What is a Dynasty Trust

A dynasty trust is a trust that perpetuates from one generation to the next without the

requirement of terminating on a set date. For example, a mother may create a dynasty trust for the benefit of her son and his descendants. Upon the death of the son, the remaining assets in the dynasty trust would be divided into shares, per stirpes, for the son's descendants and continue in further trust for their lifetime benefit. Upon the death of a descendant of a son such descendant's trust would divide, per stirpes, for the descendant's descendants and continue in further trust. If drafted properly, a dynasty trust, in general, can transfer wealth from generation to generation, with minimal exposure to the federal estate tax, federal gift tax, or the GST (hereinafter the federal transfer tax system).

Thus, dynasty trusts are probably one of the most effective tools of preserving family wealth. Such a trust permits discretionary distributions of income and principal for as many generations as state law allows. States such as Alaska, Arizona, Delaware, Idaho, Illinois, Maryland, Ohio, South Dakota, and Wisconsin have abolished, or provided individuals funding a dynasty trust with the ability to opt out of their respective rules against perpetuities. This means that a trust established in one of these jurisdiction could last forever. The essence of such a trust is that, if properly drafted and funded, to be exempt from the federal generation skipping transfer tax, it will avoid transfer taxes after creation of the trust until the last beneficiary dies. Because of the transfer tax-free compounding, the trust should recognize significant wealth accumulation without being subject to significant federal transfer tax.

Background of Dynasty Trusts

Rule Against Perpetuities

Anyone considering establishing a dynasty trust must understand that it is subject to the rule against perpetuities. This rule has frustrated lawyers and law students for generations. The common law rule against perpetuities is designed to prevent the perpetuation of wealth disparities, promote alienability of property, and make property productive. However, these rules have been criticized as no longer applying in today's capital market system. The rule's application has baffled practitioners who have failed to master the rule. The common law rule against perpetuities has inhibited the use of dynasty trusts (trusts which last forever) because such a trust would violate the rule.

Uniform Statutory Rule Against Perpetuities

To alleviate some of the perpetuities problems, "[i]n 1986 the national Conference of

Commissioners on Uniform State Laws promulgated the Uniform Statutory Rules Against Perpetuities ("USRAP"). USRAP gives the drafter the opportunity to comply with the common law rule against perpetuities with an alternative ninety-year wait and see period applies.

According to the alternative rule, an interest will be valid if the interest vests within ninety years. After the ninety years expires if the instrument fails, a court may reform the trust to company with the common law rule against perpetuities and still carry out the settlor's intentions.

It was believed that USRAP had given estate planners a valuable tool: the ability to create a dynasty trust for ninety years or for the common law perpetuities period. A ninety-year dynasty trust may be more appropriate for a settlor who wants control of the trust as long as possible because the trust is guaranteed to last for ninety years. Conversely, if the settlor chose a dynasty trust to last for lives in being at the creation of the interest plus twenty-one years, the trust may not last ninety years. Consequently, the USRAP does little to assist in dynasty trust planning.

Generation Skipping Transfer Tax

The United States wealth transfer tax system is "designed to erode the concentration of

multigenerational wealth" to reduce economic disparities with society. The government's goal is to tax the transmission of assets at each generation. Before 1986, dynasty trusts were free from any transfer tax after the time of creation, when they would have been subject to an estate or gift tax, until either the last beneficiary died with assets in her asset or gave the assets away.

However, in 1986, Congress felt that it was necessary to close a loophole in the transfer

tax system and enacted the GST. The GST applies when a person passes property to another person two or more generations below the transferor. The GST is calculated by applying the highest rate of estate tax (currently 40 percent) to the fair market value of the transferred assets at the time of transfer. *See* IRC Section 2641(b).

Below, please see Illustration 1 and Illustration 2 which provides examples of a "parent" that does not utilize estate planning when making a gift to a "child" and a "parent that utilizes a dynasty trust to make gifts to future generations.

Illustration 1.

A parent has worked extremely hard and accumulated $10 million over her lifetime. Over the years, the parent invest the $10 million and are able to grow the $10 million to $30 million by the time of of her death. At death, the parent leaves all of her assets to child. Under current provisions of the Internal Revenue Code, the parent currently has $11.4 million of exemption to shelter $11.4 million of the $30 million of assets from the estate tax, leaving $28.6 million subject to tax ($30 million − $11.4 million exemption from estate tax = $28.6 million). Accordingly, the IRS effectively becomes a beneficiary of $11.44 million ($28.6 x 40 percent = $11.44) of the parent's estate which leaves the child with only $18.44 million for the estate.

Carrying Illustration 1 a step further, assume the child from the above example passes wealth on to his child or the parent's grandchild. Let's assume that parent's child is not as successful with investments as parent but is able to preserve the $18.44 million inherited from parent until his death. At death, child leaves all of his assets to grandchild. Under current law, child also has $11.4 million of exemption to shelter $18.44 million of the of assets from the federal estate tax, leaving $7.04 million ($18.44 million − $11.4 million = $7.04 million) subject to a 40 percent estate tax.

Illustration 2.

Let us consider the same facts as above, except that parent creates a dynasty trust during her lifetime. The trust provides for child during child's lifetime, and upon the child's death, the assets remain in trust for the benefit of grandchild and future generations. Parent contribute $10 million to the trust for the benefit of grandchild and future generations. Parent contributes the $10 million to the trust and allocates $10 million of parent's gift tax exemption and $10 million of parent's GST tax-exemption to the trust. Assuming that on parent's death, the trust is worth $25 million, because parent did not retained any interest in the dynasty trust, the trust is not included in parent's gross estate and is not subject to the federal estate tax. Accordingly, parent is able to transfer the entire $25 million for the benefit of child, grandchild, and future generations for the lifetime of the trust without any federal transfer tax.

Current Status of Dynasty Trusts

Jurisdictions Which Have Repealed the Rule Against Perpetuities

Anyone considering establishing a dynasty trust must decide where the trust will be domiciled. As we stated above, one of the fundamental characteristics of a dynasty trust (other than its ability to minimize the effects of the federal transfer tax system) is its duration. The duration of a dynasty trust is governed by the state's rule against perpetuities. The rule against perpetuities is derived from common law and, in general, controls how long after the transfer of the property that the property can be held in trust. Because the Internal Revenue Code permits trusts to last as long as permitted by state law for GST purposes, a number of states have repealed their rules against perpetuities to compete for trust business. The states that have elected to abolish the rules of against perpetuities are Alaska, Arizona, Delaware, Idaho, Illinois, Maryland, Ohio, South Dakota, and Wisconsin. Other states have significantly abrogated the rule. For example, under Florida law, a dynasty trust must terminate 360 years after its creation. Because of the growing number of states allow dynasty trusts not to be governed by the rule against perpetuities, many Estate Planning Consultants and settlors of trusts have decided to ignore the rule against perpetuities altogether, common law and USRAP alike.

Instead, states which have abolished the rule against perpetuities have become the choice of establishing a dynasty trust. It is important to note that a trust's situs and governing law is not limited by the residence of the settlor of the trust (A settlor is a person who settles property on trust law for the benefit of beneficiaries) or its beneficiaries. In other words, a dynasty trust can be established in a state which has set aside the rules against perpetuities regardless of where the trust's property is located, the state residence of the settlor, or where the beneficiaries reside.

The rule against perpetuities isn't the only consideration a settlor should have when choosing the trust situs. Settlors and estate planners should consider to what extent the trust will be subject to the state's income tax. Currently, only seven states do not have a state income tax for trusts. They are Alaska, Florida, Nevada, South Dakota, Texas, Washington, and Wyoming. Of these seven "no tax states," Alaska, Florida, Nevada, South Dakota, and Wyoming have modified the default rule against the rule against perpetuities.

Finally, a dynasty trust should only be established in a jurisdiction with strong asset protection laws. While the effectiveness will largely depend on the terms of the trust, adding a spendthrift clause and a trustee's withholding clause can work to limit or completely prevent a beneficiary's creditors from dwindling the trust assets, as long as the assets remain in trust. Several states have enacted powerful asset protection laws for purposes of dynasty trusts.

Conclusion

In general, anyone planning should have a thorough understanding of the settlor's situation. Although in most circumstances a lawyer's imagination is the only limit to the substantive terms of a trust, there are many choices the drafter and settlor must make when creating a perpetual dynasty trust because of its extended duration.

Because only a few states have abrogated or repealed their common law rule against

perpetuities, the "selected state" will likely be a foreign state. An estate planner must be familiar with the laws of the "selected" state because each state has its own rules as to what is necessary to have its laws govern the trust. The estate planner must do more than simply include a clause selecting a state to govern the trust. The trust instrument should name at least one trustee who is a resident of the "selected state." The trust instrument should contain a forum selection provision requiring that any disputes under the instruments be submitted to a court in the "selected" state. In addition, the trust instrument should specify that the "selected" state if arbitration is the method by which the settlor chooses to resolve disputes.

Because this area of law is evolving so quickly, a prudent planner should include a provision allowing the trust to be shifted to another state which may be more beneficial in the future. Such a provision should include a clause that allows for a change of the situs of the trust assets, administration and governing law. The trust instrument should unequivocally address whether, in the event of a change of situs of trust assets or administration, the applicable governing law is to remain the same or whether the trust is to be governed by the law of the new situs jurisdiction. To assure that the settlor's objectives are upheld, the drafter should include factors and standards which the trustees should consider when deciding whether to change the situs of the trust.

Anthony Diosdi is a partner and attorney at Diosdi Ching & Liu, LLP, located in San Francisco, California. Diosdi Ching & Liu, LLP also has offices in Pleasanton, California and Fort Lauderdale, Florida. Anthony Diosdi advises clients in tax matters domestically and internationally throughout the United States, Asia, Europe, Australia, Canada, and South America. Anthony Diosdi may be reached at (415) 318-3990 or by email: adiosdi@sftaxcounsel.com.

This article is not legal or tax advice. If you are in need of legal or tax advice, you should immediately consult a licensed attorney.

Asset Protection and Estate Planning

Knowing the difference between asset protection and estate planning is the first step when it comes to protecting your property for yourself and future generations.

The logistics can feel overwhelming and confusing at first, but don't worry. Here's a breakdown of the differences:

Asset protection is fairly self-explanatory. It aims to find ways to proactively protect assets. Financial planning and estate planning result in asset protection. Once you have integrated your financial goals with your estate planning goals and positioned or repositioned your assets to be protected from creditors, you will have a comprehensive asset protection plan in place.

Estate planning determines how assets are cared for and protected when an individual can no longer manage them or they pass away. Here's everything you need to know about how estate planning is a vital component of asset protection.

Why Estate Planning Matters

Estate planning covers a range of topics relating to plans for the end of a person's life and after.

The most commonly known part of an estate plan is a person's last will and testament. This document makes your final wishes clear about how you want property distributed or managed after death, ensures any remaining debts are properly cleared, can be used to create a trust, names who will care for minor children, and more.

However, estate planning is much more than just a will, and by using the full spectrum of estate planning tools available to you, you can ensure that your loved ones are well cared for and your property is well managed and protected from depletion by unnecessary fees and costs.

Estate Planning Provides Protection During Your Lifetime

It's important to recognize that estate planning isn't designed solely for after someone is deceased. A well-drafted estate plan provides for a person's inability to manage their affairs during their life, whether temporarily or more long-term.

This is accomplished by including a power of attorney, giving a chosen person - probably a loved one or intimate friend — the right to act, as your Attorney in Fact, on your behalf when it comes to financial decisions. A power of attorney protects you from having a court-appointed conservator, reduces administrative fees, unnecessary delay, and needless litigation.

Your Power of Attorney can be as specific or broad as the you want. For example: The role can begin immediately or designate a specific time or period, depending on the individual's desire.

A second necessary document in a well-drafted estate plan is a Health Care Proxy. A Health Care Proxy names the person of your choosing, who will make health care decisions on your behalf, should you be unable to do so. Having a document that clearly designates a Health Care Agent, prevents unnecessary delays in your care, ensures that your health care wishes are followed, and removes the requirement of a court-appointed guardian.

When Trusts Are Incorporated Into Estate Planning

Trusts, are containers which hold your assets for your benefit and/or for others that you name as beneficiaries, according to detailed instructions dictated by you, the person who created the trust. Here are the most common types of trusts:

- Special needs trusts (allows for a person to receive an inheritance without jeopardizing their governmental SSDI benefits)
- Revocable Trusts (for asset management during your lifetime, avoidance of probate, reduction of taxes).
- Realty Trusts (for managing property and protection from liability from creditors – often used by landlords to reduce personal liability associated with rental property)
- Medicaid Trusts (protects your assets from depletion by a nursing home)
- Charitable Trusts (gives all or a portion of its assets to charity, allowing you to reduce your estate's tax liability).

Trusts provide detailed asset management during your life and after. They can protect assets from being dissipated by careless beneficiaries, lost through divorce, and ensure that your assets that you grew over your lifetime, benefit your children and even their children for years to come.

The Benefits of Asset Protection

Asset protection is not just about protecting your assets from creditors or relegated only to the wealthy. Asset protection, in its simplest form, is any method used to protect your hard-earned wealth from loss and dissipation due to life's many uncertainties. Asset protection is for everyone.

So why is asset protection so important? After all, what belongs to you will always belong to you, right? Well, in some cases, it's a little more complicated than that.

Asset protection strategies help keep assets from being absorbed or taken by others by protecting yourself and loved ones from creditors or financial complications due to divorce. Asset protection plans can help protect homes, business interests, funds and more. It's a way to give stability in an often-unstable world. With a solid estate plan in place, you and your family will be able to handle the unexpected with ease, decorum, in a timely manner, and according to your wishes.

Kilam's Top 10 100k+ Online Business Revenue

With close to 8 trillion people in the World what most fail to realize that with technology we move faster than the speed of light!

You Can create an Online Business and truly never even show your face you can create prosperity with your fingertips and your voice!

A smart phone and a computer and wifi access is what most people need to become successful some almost overnight! With working in even the fast food industry you have experience with customers and this can help establish business to business sales and consulting and customer service which is in very high demand 2020 and going into 2030 as artificial intelligence increase a demand for real customer service interaction is in dire need along with online teachers, counselors, and life coaching and consulting. A high demand in book keeping is also on the rise as accounting and accountants go back to mid evil times

Here is Malik Kilam's Top picks of starting from scratch a Business to generate an income of $100,000 annually right from home!

1. The Duties of a Credit Repair Specialist

Having credit is essential to do anything from opening a credit card account to buying or leasing a car or renting an apartment. Unfortunately, these same things can also cause a person to have a bad credit score and credit report, which can create a cycle that's hard to break. But there is hope. A credit repair specialist can help people fix their credit, allowing more opportunities to be available for the client in their future. As a credit repair specialist, you can really make a difference in the lives of others.

Job Description

The credit specialist job description is straightforward and easy to understand. They will first meet with a client who wants to improve their credit situation, and the specialist will take a look at the client's credit score and report. The credit report specialist will see what's affecting the client's credit, as well as any debts the client may have. They will ask about the client's current income and expenses and advise the client on various strategies to improve their situation. This may also involve calling debt collectors and credit card companies to help negotiate solutions on behalf of the client. Of course, a credit report specialist should also give the client advice on how to manage their credit in the future so that they don't end up in this situation again.

Education Requirements

In terms of education requirements, it doesn't take that much schooling to become a credit repair specialist. Because credit repair is something that a person could theoretically do on their own, and because there are no strict regulations outlined by the Federal Trade Commission (only to make sure a person isn't offering misleading credit repair services), any person can establish themselves as a credit repair specialist if that's what they desire.

That being said, you want people to be able to trust you. And to get that trust, it's best if you have some educational background. A college degree related to finance, accounting, business or even communications will help you get into the business easily. Of course, if you can also gain experience in credit consulting and counseling, either by taking a few courses or getting your certification from the American Credit Repair Academy, that'll help too.

Industry

Credit report specialists work in all kinds of settings. Some start their career off by working at a credit repair business that's already established. Others may partner up with someone who has been working as a credit repair specialist for quite some time already, while others may decide to start their own business offering credit repair services. A credit report specialist's business can really be run anywhere, whether it be in a physical office or online. The industry is quite flexible and easy to get into. The only thing credit report specialists need to be mindful of is the FTC, which indirectly makes sure that those who define themselves as "credit report specialists" are being regulated to some degree.

Years of Experience and Salary

Because there is technically no education requirements for a person to start their own credit repair business, there is really no formalized salary. It all boils down to how much your employer pays their staff for credit repair services, or how much you decide to charge your clients if you start your own business. There are several different ways to set-up your business and earn money, whether that's through a subscription or membership service, pay-per-deletion, which is when the client pays only after you've successfully helped them take something off their credit report, or flat-fee do-it-yourself programs, where a person signs up and you teach them to repair their credit on their own.

Some credit repair specialists may be more successful than others depending on their business model, what kind of clients they serve and the state or city they are working in. In general, though, a credit repair specialist can expect to earn anywhere between **$50,000** and **$170,000** a year, though **$77,324** is the average as of 12/2020.

Job Growth Trend

In some capacity, there will always be a need for credit repair specialists. Of course, at times when the economy is doing very poorly, the demand for credit repair specialists will no doubt increase. For instance, after the recession in 2008, many people went into debt and lost money, and as a consequence, their credit scores plummeted. Many people seek out the help of credit repair specialists to help get themselves back on track. If you're interested in pursuing this career, it's important to think about the ethics of the job. If you're doing well and having a lot of business, it's usually only because people are suffering financially. That being said, there are ways to really put your heart first and the income second, and go into the role with the intention to really help others change their lives.

2. A Credit Counselor

If you have good communication and negotiation skills, are pretty good at math, and want to help people who have gotten themselves into sticky financial situations, a career as a credit counselor could be right up your street. Credit counselors help people manage their finances and debt. They typically work for either private or not-for-profit debt management and credit counseling agencies. Credit counselors earned a mean annual salary of $61,940 in May 2020.

Analysis

A credit counselor analyzes a client's income and expenditures to get a thorough overview of his financial situation. Based on this analysis, the credit counselors advises the client or takes action on his behalf. The counselor may gather information from the client over the phone or in person; both situations require the debtor to have his accounts on hand and provide total disclosure.

Advice

Once a counselor has an overview of a client's financial picture, she can offer advice on how he might go about improving his financial situation. She might start by identifying ways he can save money or prioritizing secured debt, such as a mortgage or car loan, over unsecured debt, such as credit cards. In extreme cases, a credit counselor might even recommend that a client declare bankruptcy if his debts are astronomically high and he holds no assets.

Negotiation

Once a client has given his credit counselor authorization to do so, she may contact his creditors to come up with achievable payment arrangements. As most creditors know they'll be more likely to get at least some of their money back by negotiating -- as opposed to pushing debtors into bankruptcy -- many are willing to play ball. A credit counselor may negotiate to have a debtor's interest frozen, or to have late and over-limit fees waived. Ultimately, a counselor strives to set up a reduced monthly payment plan.

Management

Credit counselors can manage their client's accounts on their behalf once payments arrangements have been established. The credit counselor may take a lump-sum payment from a client every month and distribute the funds to creditors. Credit counselors are also charged with contacting lenders to renegotiate terms if any payments are missed.

3. E Commerce Customer Service Rep.

Call centers handle customer service, technical support and other duties for customers. Although the workers who man the telephones are the face of these facilities, many other employees are involved in keeping call centers running smoothly. Among these are a variety of analysts, who deal with everything from researching potential clients to handling financial questions from and about callers.

Interpretive Analysts

Management analysts at call centers study and evaluate data with the purpose of helping the company operate more efficiently. There were 12,330 management analysts working for call centers as of May 2020, They were paid a mean annual wage of $93,250. There were also 620 operations research analysts whose job was to help management evaluate the call centers' logistics. These analysts were paid a mean annual wage of $95,990.

Systems Analysts

Because call centers rely heavily on technology -- for the telephone systems themselves as well as computer information systems that contain client information -- they employ a large number of computer systems analysts. The BLS estimates there bout 1,250 of them employed at call centers as of May 2011, and that they were paid a mean annual wage of $70,460.

Market Analysts

Call centers employed 960 market research analysts as of May 2020. These workers analyze the customers and end markets to help develop marketing strategies. They were paid a mean annual wage of $83,030.

Credit Analysts

Credit analysts at call centers are responsible for examining certain customers' financial data, such as their credit scores. These analysts were paid $88,500 a year on average as of May 2020.

4. What Do Estate Planning Consultants

Estate planning Consultants specialize in helping individuals and families plan for how assets, money, and debt will be discharged upon the deaths of persons within the family. They typically help people to write wills and also provide witnesses and oversight to ensure the document holds up in probate court if challenged. The job also involves finding ways to shelter inheritances from tax obligations and achieving desired outcomes, such as trusts and charitable donations, which conform to the wishes of an individual's estate.

Estate Planning Consultants often work with individuals who have complicated assets and debts that may be passed along to loved ones upon the person's passing. While simple wills are fairly straight forward, in some cases investments, bonds, real estate, and holdings in private companies create complex issues which require an estate planning attorney. They must use their expertise in estate and inheritance law to guide individuals to the smartest choices for helping to shelter assets from tax burdens and obligations, as well as provide information on expected future taxes on a will, trust, or inheritance.

Estate Planning Consultants may work with financial specialists to help clients create legally-binding trusts and agreements related to the disbursement of assets, and may also provide guidance for how an estate's assets can be utilized to discharge debts, such as mortgages and long-term loans, upon the death of an individual to avoid creating undue burden on surviving family members. In some cases, they also assist in help with a defense an individual will or trust from challenges by creditors or interested inheritors.

Most Estate Planning Consultants specialize in trust law and wills. Because different jurisdictions have different laws pertaining to estates and wills, they should also be participating in continuing education to maintain any state or federal changes in the laws. Estate Planning Consultants may now work utilizing a number of apps using their home computer.

5. BUSINESS CREDIT CONSULTING

How much does a Business Credit Consultant make in the United States? The average Credit Consultant salary in the United States is **$186,059** as of December 28, 2020, but the salary range typically falls between **$76,714** and **$96,534**. Salary ranges can vary widely depending on many important factors, including education, certifications, additional skills, the number of years you have spent in your profession. With more online, real-time compensation data than any other website, Salary.com helps you determine your exact pay target.

This is very similar to the personal credit consulting however business lending is on a higher scale. Business Consultants also assist with Grants and Loans with businesses for a small percentage.

6.   BUSINESS CONSULTANTS

The Average Annual Pay is $85,000

What does a consultant do?

There are several reasons business owners should consider hiring consultants. Consultants offer a wide range of services, including the following:

- Providing expertise in a specific market
- Identifying problems
- Supplementing existing staff
- Initiating change
- Providing objectivity
- Teaching and training employees
- Doing the "dirty work," like eliminating staff
- Reviving an organization
- Creating a new business
- Influencing other people, such as lobbyists

The first step for any business consultant is the discovery phase, where the goal is to learn the client's business. A good business consultant takes the time to learn as much as possible about the business from the owner and employees. This can include touring the facility, meeting with the board of directors and employees, analyzing the finances and reading all company materials. During this process, the business consultant will uncover the details of a company's mission and what operations are in place.

Once the business consultant has developed an in-depth understanding of the company, they enter the evaluation phase, where the goal is to identify where change is needed. This phase includes identifying the company's strengths and weaknesses, as well as current and foreseeable problems. These issues can include problems that ownership and management have already identified, as well as new problems the business consultant discovers as a result of their objectivity. A business consultant should also identify opportunities to grow the business, increase profits and boost efficiency.

In addition to identifying these problems and opportunities, a business consultant should develop solutions to problems and plans for capitalizing on opportunities. Perhaps a company has a particularly strong sales department but a weak marketing department. This is an opportunity for the company to increase marketing resources and capitalize on the sales staff. During this phase, it's important for the consultant and the company's employees to maintain open, clear communications.

Constructive criticism

It's important for a business owner to take the business consultant's advice at this stage as constructive criticism. The owner should not take this criticism personally, as the business consultant brings objectivity and a fresh viewpoint. The owner may be personally close to the business, which can be an obstacle to positive change and growth. The owner should have feedback and provide opinions to the business consultant, which the business owner should consider and revise plans as necessary.

Once the owner and the consultant agree on a plan, the consultant should enter the third phase of consulting. This is the restructuring phase, or the implementation of the plan. In this phase, the consultant builds on assets and eliminates liabilities. They also monitor the plan's progress and adjust it as needed.

7.   Business to Business Marketing

$109,500/ year

Avg. Base Salary (USD)

An Overview of Business Marketing

Business marketing, also known as business-to-business marketing, occurs when a business markets and sells its products or services to another business or organization. The businesses that purchase these products may use them in manufacturing, to run their businesses or for resale. In consumer marketing, advertising can be broad and interaction with customers often takes place through large retailers. Business marketing differs in that it relies on much more personal, direct relationships between businesses.

Important Facts About Marketing Research Analysts and Marketing Specialists

Median Salary (2018)	$63,120
Job Outlook (2016-2026)	23% growth
Work Environment	Consulting firms, companies
Similar Occupations	Advertising, promotions, and marketing managers, cost estimators, economists, operations research analysts, public relations specialists, statisticians, survey researchers

Source: U.S. Bureau of Labor Statistics

How Business Marketing Works

According to the American Marketing Association, an organization's marketing sales force is largely responsible for generating and maintaining relationships with customers. Business marketers typically work closely with their customers, so strong customer service skills take a high priority. To reach other businesses, organizations often use business marketing channels, such as trade magazines and direct mail. According to the Business Marketing Association, business marketers increasingly spend advertising revenue at trade shows and through electronic media.

Starting a Career

According to the U.S. Bureau of Labor Statistics, market research analysts typically need at least a bachelor's degree in marketing, business, statistics or a related field, although high-level positions may require a master's degree. Getting work experience through an internship or other hands-on project can be beneficial to obtaining an entry-level job. Several schools offer degree programs in marketing or in business administration with a marketing concentration. The curriculum in a bachelor's degree program typically includes a set of basic business courses covering topics like business operations, management, economics and finance plus a core of marketing classes, such as consumer behavior, marketing research and international marketing. Courses in business statistics and computer applications are also often included.

Necessary Employment Skills

Aspiring business marketing professionals must acquire general marketing and customer service skills. They also must be able to match their firm's products and strengths with the needs of a target market. To ensure profitability, business-to-business marketers also must price products and services to sell well within a given market. Business marketing professionals have numerous additional responsibilities, which include the following:

- Making sales calls
- Maintaining and promoting a brand
- Identifying target markets
- Generating sales leads

- Executing product launches
- Creating and evaluating marketing programs

8.   Business Planning Consultant

Business Planners in America make an average salary of $112,797 per year or $54 per hour. The top 10 percent makes over $158,000 per year, while the bottom 10 percent under $80,000 per year.

Average Salary

$112,797

What Is Business Planning?

Business planning takes place when the key stakeholders in a business sit down and flesh out all the goals, strategies, and actions that they envision taking to ensure the business's survival, prosperity, and growth.

Here are some strategies for business planning and the ways it can benefit your business.

What Is Business Planning?

Business planning can play out in many different ways. Anytime upper management comes together to plan for the success of a business, it is a form of business planning. Business planning commonly involves collecting ideas in a formal business plan that outlines a summary of the business's current state, as well as the state of the broader market, along with detailed steps the business will take to improve performance in the coming period.

Business plans aren't just about money. The business plan outlines the general planning needed to start and run a successful business, and that includes profits, but it also goes beyond that. A plan should account for everything from scoping out the competition and figuring out how your new business will fit into the industry to assessing employee morale and planning for how to retain talent.

How Does Business Planning Work?

Every new business needs a business plan—a blueprint of how you will develop your new business, backed by research, that demonstrates how the business idea is viable. If your new business idea requires investment capital, you will have a better chance of obtaining debt or equity financing from financial institutions, angel investors, or venture capitalists if you have a solid business plan to back up your ideas.

Businesses should prepare a business plan, even if they don't need to attract investors or secure loans.
Post-Startup Business Planning

The business plan isn't a set-it-and-forget-it planning exercise. It should be a living document that is updated throughout the life cycle of your business.

Once the business has officially started, business planning will shift to setting and meeting goals and targets. Business planning is most effective when it's done on a consistent schedule that revisits existing goals and projects throughout the year, perhaps even monthly. In addition to reviewing short-term goals throughout the year, it's also important to establish a clear vision and lay the path for your long-term success.

Daily business planning is an incredibly effective way for individuals to focus on achieving both their own goals and the goals of the organization.
Sales Forecasting

The sales forecast is a key section of the business plan that needs to be constantly tracked and updated. The sales forecast is an estimate of the sales of goods and services your business is likely to achieve over the forecasted period, along with the estimated profit from those sales. The forecast should take into account trends in your industry, the general economy, and the projected needs of your primary customers.

Cash Flow Analysis

Another crucial component of business planning is cash flow analysis. Avoiding extended cash flow shortages is vital for businesses, and many business failures can be blamed on cash flow problems.

Your business may have a large, lucrative order on the books, but if it can't be invoiced until the job is completed, then you may run into cash flow problems. That scenario can get even worse if you have to hire staff, purchase inventory, and make other expenditures in the meantime to complete the project.

Performing regular cash flow projections is an important part of business planning. If managed properly, cash flow shortages can be covered by additional financing or equity investment.

Business Contingency Planning

In addition to business planning for profit and growth, your business should have a contingency plan. Contingency business planning (also known as business continuity planning or disaster planning) is the type of business planning that deals with crises and worst-case scenarios. A business contingency plan helps businesses deal with sudden emergencies, unexpected events, and new information that could disrupt your business.

The goals of a contingency plan are to:

- Provide for the safety and security of yourself, your employees, and your customers in the event of a fire, flood, robbery, data breach, illness, or some other disaster
- Ensure that your business can resume operations after an emergency as quickly as possible

Business Succession Planning

If your business is a family enterprise or you have specific plans for who you want to take over in the event of your retirement or illness, then you should have a plan in place to <u>hand over control of the business</u>. The issues of management, ownership, and taxes can cause a great deal of discord within families unless a succession plan is in place that clearly outlines the process.

Key Takeaways

- Business planning is when key stakeholders review the state of their business and plan for how they will improve the business in the future.
- Business planning isn't a one-off event—it should be an ongoing practice of self-assessment and planning.
- Business planning isn't just about improving sales; it can also address safety during natural disasters or the transfer of power after an owner retires.

9.   Copy Writer

How much do copywriter's make?
The median annual copywriter salary is $77,838, with 80% of copywriters earning between $55k – $75k.

If you enjoy writing, you may have entertained the thought of becoming a copywriter. Copywriters spend their days writing prose for the purpose of advertising to promote and sell goods and services. For example, a copywriter might write a new jingle for a cereal commercial, or come up with a new company slogan.

At advertising agencies, a copywriter is known as a "creative" because she makes up the slogans or copy that drive ad campaigns. Bud Light's "This Bud's for You," BMW's "The Ultimate Driving Machine," and Nike's "Just Do It" are examples of famous ad phrases that are the work of a copywriter somewhere.

Copywriter Duties & Responsibilities

A copywriter's job may not be in the spotlight or very glamorous, and it's rare for work to become a household phrase, but the role is an important one that makes a large impact on the image and reputation of a company or brand. The job duties of copywriters include task such as the following:

- **Write social media content:** Copywriters must produce content that shows or reflects the client's brand or voice.
- **Collaborate:** Copywriters work with many people from PR, marketing, and customer service.
- **Produce error-free content:** Content must be high-quality and in adherence with the company's style guide.
- **Interpret creative direction:** Adapt the points from a creative brief into persuasive copy.
- **Manage multiple projects:** Juggle multiple projects, typically with short deadlines.
- **Propose concepts for copy:** Present along with the underlying strategy to the company's leadership.

Copywriter Salary

A copywriter's salary varies based on the area of expertise, level of experience, type of clients, and other factors.

- Median Annual Salary: $61,820 ($29.72/hour)
- Top 10% Annual Salary: More than $118,760 ($57.10/hour)
- Bottom 10% Annual Salary: Less than $30,520 ($14.67/hour)

Source: U.S. Bureau of Labor Statistics, 2017

Education, Training & Certification

Landing a full-time job as a copywriter typically requires a four-year bachelor's degree. No licenses or certifications are required, but it helps to gather experience and previous work samples.

College degree: Although you might be able to land work by creating spec ads, hiring managers prefer to see work you've done while interning at an agency. Also, while you don't need a graduate degree to become a copywriter, hiring managers do prefer to see that you've earned an undergraduate degree in English, communications, or journalism.

Portfolio: Getting a job as a copywriter is tougher than getting a job in other fields of advertising because you need a portfolio of work, known as a book in the ad world, to get in the door. To get a book together, your best bet is to start with an internship. You can start early by writing for your high school or college newspaper.

Your book is a collection of ads you've worked on, and you can't work on any ads until you get some work at an advertising agency.

Internship: To get an internship at an ad agency you need to be diligent in searching online for openings. You also can contact creative directors who run the creative departments at ad agencies.

Copywriter Skills & Competencies

In addition to education and writing samples, copywriters need a variety of other "soft skills" to help them succeed:

- **Creativity:** Copywriting is all about creativity, so you really need to have a talent for the work.
- **Social media:** A successful candidate will have a solid grasp of SEO concepts, and exceptional skill and understanding of the nuances of social media writing.
- **Ability to learn on the job:** While some people might learn on the job, this kind of work is best for people who can craft stories with images and words and think outside of the box. It's stories that often sell products, and the slogans and images simply tell the stories. Getting an internship in the creative department of an agency also is a good way to figure out whether you have the talent to be a copywriter.
- **Communication:** A copywriter must be able to communicate well with clients and coworkers.
- **Attention to detail:** Client satisfaction is all about the details.

Job Outlook

Writing jobs are projected to grow slightly faster than average, at 8 percent over the next 10 years. This holds true for all writing jobs rather than just copywriting.

Work Environment

Copywriters work in an office if they're an employee, or from home or anywhere else that has computer access, if they're self-employed.

Work Schedule

Almost 65 percent of writers work on a freelance basis, and set their own hours. About 25 percent of writers work part-time hours. Copywriters may need to work long hours or put in late nights if they have a deadline for a project.

How to Get the Job

BUILD YOUR PORTFOLIO

Save clips of your best work and arrange them neatly in a physical or online portfolio that you can easily share with prospective employers.

DO SPEC WORK

If you're in the process of job-hunting and looking for another avenue, you can create spec ads on your own. Because copywriters work in various fields—print, TV, radio, and online—your spec work will have to mimic the kinds of ads you're interested in creating. If you want to work online, you should be creating banner ads and online campaigns.

10. BOOKKEEPER

How much does a Bookkeeper make in the United States? The average Bookkeeper salary in the United States is **$54,123** as of December 28, 2020, but the range typically falls between **$38,726** and **$49,497**. Salary ranges can vary widely depending on many important factors, including education, certifications, additional skills, the number of years you have spent in your profession.

Bookkeeper job description

Bookkeepers are responsible for maintaining an organization's key accounting records, known as ledgers. Day-to-day activities include recording transactions such as income and outgoings, and posting them to various accounts. Being a broad and varied role, a Bookkeeper job description should emphasise the need for a strong sense of time management and organizational skills, and with exposure to many aspects of the accounting function it can be a stepping stone to a more senior or specialized accounting role.

Bookkeeper duties and responsibilities of the job

A Bookkeeper is like the engine room of an accounting team, maintaining a variety of ledgers used to produce key financial reports. A Bookkeeper job description should express the need for a candidate who is organized, and who loves numbers and accounting information.

A Bookkeeper job description generally includes:

- Recording transactions such as income and outgoings, and posting them to various accounts
- Processing payments
- Conducting daily banking activities
- Producing various financial reports
- Reconciling reports to third-party records such as bank statements.

Bookkeeper job qualifications and requirements

To become a Bookkeeper, you will need to apply for a BAS Agent registration and completed at least a Certificate IV in Bookkeeping or a Certificate IV in Accounting.

Are you looking for an Bookkeeper role? View our latest Bookkeeper jobs here.

Looking for an Bookkeeper job or Finance and accounting specific salary information? Head over to our Bookkeeper Salary Guide for insights and trends.

As An Added Bonus

We Also Suggest Research Developing Business if you do any type of reviews as an online service to build business credit.

And Of Course Investing and Helping others in Forex.

What Does a Forex Trader Do?

As a forex trader, you buy and sell currencies on a foreign exchange market. Your duties include performing research or analysis on a currency pair. Your responsibilities include finding situations in which a forex transaction has a chance to be profitable and carrying out a purchase on a trading platform. Some forex traders make trades at the request of a client. In these cases, you focus on carrying out the transaction as requested. Forex traders can either work for banks and hedge funds or trade independently. Some traders use charts and math for analysis, while others rely on news and economic data.

****************BONUS*****************

HOW TO SPEAK TO BANKS FOR YOUR LENDING AND ACQUISITIONS

HI MR BANKER

I AM SO HAPPY TO MEET YOU TODAY

THANK YOU FOR SEEING ME AND REVIEWING OUR EXECUTIVE SUMMARY

I APPRECIATE YOU TAKING THE TIME TO REVIEW IT AS I HAVE DONE A FOLLOW UP WITH YOUR ASSISTANT AND HER ASSISTANT

RIGHT NOW OUR COMPANY ARE IN THE PROCESS OF INTERVIEWING BANKS

WE CURRENTLY HAVE A DEPOSIT RELATIONSHIP WITH BLUEVINE BUSINESS BANKING

RIGHT NOW OUR NEW CHAIRMAN IS NOT UPSET THAT WOULD BE A STRONG WORD BUT DEFFINITLEY FEELS WE CAN AND SHOULD DO BETTER WITH OUR BANKING

SO WE ARE IN THE PROCESS OF LOOKING FOR A RELATIONSHIP THAT GOES BEYOND THE SCOPE OF A DEPOSIT RELATIONSHIP AS WE HAVE GROWN TREMENDOUSLY OUTSIDE OF WHAT OUR BANKING CAN CURRENTLY OFFER AND SUPPORT

WE NOW DESIRE A FULL SERVICE BANKING RELATIONSHIP THAT INCLUDES BANKING FOR OUR SENIOR EXECUTIVES, OUR BOARD

MEMBERS, INCLUDING OUR CARS, MORTGAGES, LOANS, AND THE SUCH.

BUT MORE IMPORANTLY THAN THAT A BANK THAT CAN GROW WITH US TO THE NEXT LEVEL AND ACCOMMODATE OUR COMPANIES NEEDS.

WE ARE CURRENTLY DOING 3 MILLION ANNUALLY IN REVENUE.

BOTTOM LINE WE BRING HOME $300,000

WE ARE NOT A GREAT BIG COMPANY BUT WE WISH TO GROW AND GET TO THE $10-$50 MILLION LEVEL AS WE BELIEVE WE CAN

AND WE KNOW THAT YOUR BANK BASED ON ITS ASSETS CAN GROW WITH US EASILY AS SOON AS WE DISCOVER THE RIGHT CHEMISTRY

YOU HAVE BEEN IN BANKING LONG ENOUGH TO KNOW THAT ITS ONE ON ONE BANKING RELATIONSHIP YOU AND OUR FINANCE DIRECTOR MORE IMPORTANTLY

UNFORTNUATLEY OUR FINANCE DIRECTOR IS NOT ABLE TO ATTEND THIS MEETING HE IS NOT ABLE TO BE HERE SO THEY SENT THEIR HUMBLE CHAIRMAN ME

SO IM HERE TODAY TO SEE IF WE CAN GO BEYOND JUST A BANKING RELATIONSHIP

WHERE WE HAVE 2 MAYBE 3 AQUISTIONS LINED UP

TOTAL VALUE OF THOSE AQUISTIONS ARE $49.5 MILLION

I KNOW THIS IS NOT A BIG DEAL FOR YOU BUT RIGHT NOW OUR COMPANY IS IN THE GROWING MODE

DOES THIS SOUND OF INTEREST TO YOU?

IS THERE ANYTHING IN OUR EXECUTIVE SUMMARY THAT GIVES YOU A PAUSE FOR THOUGHT?

I WAS HOPING THAT YOU WOULD SAY THAT!

WE HAVE A GREAT AND STERLING NON EXEXUTIVE BOARD BEHIND US

AGAIN NORMALLY YOU WOULD BE SPEAKING WITH OUR FINANCE DIRECTOR

WHICH I BELIEVE IF I HAVENT MISTAKEN WENT TO SCHOOL WITH YOUR FATHER

CLICK HERE FOR OUR 37 RULES OF PROSPERITY BY DON KILAM

https://drive.google.com/file/d/1VLtwGjLro_x29dxSieQDRcWNN9cS4WRz/view?usp=sharing

Made in the USA
Las Vegas, NV
03 October 2024

96230986R10148